Lesbian Erotica

A Hot Lesbian College BDSM Relationship

Truman Green

The previous time, I believe I got a bit carried away. I swear, I don't talk only about sex. I can only concentrate on that right now. I'm curious about your interests and activities. How close are you to your family? What is your preferred cuisine? Do you prefer the beach or the mountains? Pop or country music? I'm eager to learn all of those things and more. What information about me do you want to know? Oh, I see. You must wait till you determine when to terminate the game and meet before you ask me anything.

The last time I saw you, you were wearing green once again, but there was no blue bracelet. I really believe you are on the verge of caving in. I can see that you are once again vigilantly searching your surroundings for me.

I'm wondering if there's anything I can do to make things go more quickly. I must confess that I shall miss our current little game of mystery and suspense. There is always a potential that you may catch me gazing for an extended period of time, and I never know when you might decide it's time for me to come out.

What do you anticipate our meeting to be like? It will probably be uncomfortable at first. You'll attempt to assess me by sneaking glances while avoiding detection, like I have done during the last several weeks. However, I will finally be allowed to stare at you without being concerned about being seen. When you start to grin, I like seeing how your lips start to curve at the corners. I'll try to get you to chuckle. Your grin has the power to engulf me. It is very loving and sincere.

We may meet at one of the movie theater's afternoon matinees so we can get to know one another without anxious small talk and uncomfortable silence. No, unless you like to do it in public places, I'm not attempting to keep you in the dark so I can move in. I'm just kidding.

We might go to supper after the movie and start the customary marathon of questions and answers.

Last night, I had a dream about you. It was the evening's conclusion and we had previously met. I extended an invitation for us to continue talking in my house. As you sat behind the bar across from me, I brewed coffee. I was unprepared for the return of the anxiety I had experienced earlier in the evening. I enjoyed our time together so far, and I felt the same way about you, but it didn't make me feel less anxious.

With my back to you, I pretended to be busy in an effort to mask how agitated I felt. I turned to face you when the coffee was completed brewing, unsure whether you were still there because neither of us had struck up a conversation. You sat up straight on your stool, and I grinned. Although I couldn't be certain, I got the impression that you were gazing at me and weren't aware that I was now facing you. You flushed and inhaled deeply as you raised your eyes to meet mine. You didn't attempt to cover your view of the front of my shirt as you let your eyes stray to the ground, so I leaned over the countertop conscious of this. What do you think about it? I queried.

Again standing up straight, uncertainty was evident on your face. "I apologize. What do you like how?

I made my way back to the coffee maker. "I want coffee. Do you want it robust and black or sweet and creamy? In anticipation of your response, I set your cup down in front of you.

"Sweet. I licked the coffee off my thumb that had spilled as I brought it across the kitchen and you said, "I prefer it sweet. I saw how little it prompted you to adjust your posture, and for extra impact, I licked the area on my thumb. I set the sugar and liquid creamer in front of you. Saying, "Here you go."

I entered the living room past you, went around the counter, and sat down on one end of the sofa. Before turning back, you took your time adding the ingredients to your cup. You were deciding whether to remain where you were or venture to join me on the sofa, and I could see you doing this. "Move closer. I can assure you that it is far more comfy than that stiff stool. Before setting the spoon on a napkin on the counter, you gave the mixture one more swirl and licked it.

I slowly sipped my drink as I waited for you to move closer to me or to the other end of the sofa. You made the choice to divide the distance in half. I made a 180-degree spin to face you. My mind wandered off on its own as I saw your fingers holding the cup while having filthy thoughts. We each clung to our coffee mugs in the uncomfortable stillness, wondering what the other was thinking.

I made the decision to end the discomfort as soon as I realized that you were really seated on my sofa. I found myself fixed on you. You were stunning. I was much more attracted to you after learning more about you over dinner. You were thoughtful, humble, hospitable, sympathetic, and kind. I could have reached you with my arm, but I refrained. I have definitely improved over the last several weeks, by

God. I didn't want to do anything to mess things up at this point.

When you saw that I was looking at you, you hesitantly smiled back at me. I saw you inhale deeply and slowly exhale, allowing your muscles to relax and the stress to go away. You turned to face me while kicking off your shoes and raising your legs off the sofa. For you to face me, there was a full turn, not just a little one. In reaction, I moved a little farther and put my right arm over the couch's back. Like you, I crossed my legs in front of me and placed my coffee cup on my left knee.

We still hadn't discussed the reasons we were there, what I had told you, or anything else that may have brought us here. Dinner was more like a blind date when we got to know one other better. You were hesitant to let me let you set the pace, but I was still eager to do so. "So, am I the one who is crazy for pursuing you the way I did, or should I be worried that you responded?" I queried.

With that smile that has made me weak in the knees for months, you grinned at me. You bowed your head and made a little movement. Knowing that I had caused you pain made me cringe. You turned to face me again. "Perhaps we're both a little crazy,"

Realizing that I had tightened my jaw in anticipation of your response, I released it. "You could be correct, but I can't be held responsible for trying. On the other hand, I don't know anything about you. Perhaps I should be the one concerned because you seemed so at ease meeting a total stranger. I winked while grinning.

You relaxedly rested your elbow on the couch's back. Hey, with all those letters you taunted me and made it fascinating. How could I resist the need to meet my enigmatic admirer?

"Oh, you think I teased you? How are you doing? With those costumes, you were the one driving me nuts. Your attempts to entice me were successful. The tease was on you. After seeing you, I was unable to focus on anything for the remainder of the day.

But I was the one who was clueless about your appearance and identity. With those messages and hints, you almost sent me over the brink, so I retaliated in the only manner I knew how. While still tempting me, you ran your fingers through your hair while being conscious of what you were doing.

Then, I suppose we're even. I stood because I had to go. Are you ready for me to take that? I questioned while pointing at your cup. You gave me it after nodding. I found you rubbing your hands on your pants when I got back from the kitchen. I also saw that the top of your bra was visible since you had undone a few more buttons on your shirt. I forced a firm swallow while rubbing the back of my neck. I sat down with you again, this time closer to you on the sofa. I turned to face you with one knee curled under me, just brushing yours. When you felt the light touch, you glanced down.

I watched as your eyes followed my hand as I laid my hand on your leg just above the knee. The muscles underneath tensed for the tiniest fraction of a second before releasing once again. So, I hope that meeting me wasn't a letdown. I allowed my fingers to creep up and caress your thigh even though I was aware that you had not yet turned to look at me.

You gave a throat clearing and raised your head till our eyes matched. "Uh, no. Absolutely no disappointment.

I scooted a little closer till my knee was beneath yours, leaning my upper body further towards you. "That nearly sounded plausible. Do I cause you any discomfort?

As I drew nearer to you, you fixed your gaze on my waist before tracing your gaze upward and stopping on my lips. I licked my bottom lip as I waited for you to speak while I was conscious of your attention. I believe I could feel the heat seeping through your pants as your cheeks reddened. "I'm good. I don't feel uneasy. Despite your voice cracking, you responded, "You don't make me feel uneasy.

As I drew nearer to you until you were practically sitting in my lap, I slipped my hand up your leg and started making long, slow strokes up and down it from hip to knee. That was even less persuasive than your first response, I thought. You will need to do better than that. What about warm? You seem hot.

Before you could stop it, a little sigh came from your mouth. You tensed up once again, but then you turned to face me. "I am heated, yes. You're hot, I mean. You see, you're hot to me. You attempted to cover your face with your hands while shaking your head.

Your hands were on my thighs when I yanked them away, kissing the backs of your knuckles. I wasn't sure whether you would slide them up more, but instead you pulled me in closer by using the belt loops on my trousers. My lips curled into a broad grin. "Much better; that was stronger evidence." You had barely moistened your lips with your tongue when I peered down at them. As my pulse beat rapidly in my chest, I came closer to you and kissed your nose. Your chest's movement matched mine in rising and falling. While I felt your warm breath on my lips in anticipation of a kiss, I relished the buildup too much to give in just yet.

In an effort to press my lips into yours, your hands trailed up my sides and up to my neck. As you stroked your fingers through my hair, my heart began to rush. I moved to sit with my back against the sofa and dragged you on top of me so that you were straddling my lap. To prevent you from passing me, I firmly put my hands on your hips, but it did not stop you from slamming into me. I started kissing your bare breast flesh and worked my way up to your neck as I felt your pulse pick up between my lips. Where your shoulder curled to meet your neck, I gave it a little nip. You sighed, so I repeated brushing the area with my teeth while making a note to come back to it later.

I found myself looking up at you when you tugged on my hair enough to make me tilt my head back. As you fixedly looked back at me, your skin became even more rose. I joined in with you, and now I'm sitting on your lap. To emphasize your point, you shifted your pelvis closer to my waist. Is this the conclusion? Do you want to continue performing tricks to escape my kiss? You slowly teased by unbuttoning the remaining buttons on your shirt one at a time. Or are we going to see where this goes if we complete it?

My words failed me. Yes, it was a touch corny, but for some reason it seemed so much more seductive when you were sitting in my lap and taking off your clothing while repeating those words, particularly coming from the breathy whisper escaping between your lovely lips. You leaned down and yanked my shirt over my head before I could raise my voice to respond. When I came to my senses, I managed to remark, "Let's finish this." I went back to the pleasure spot I had discovered earlier near your neck, and I pressed your hips tightly against mine. Before putting my forehead to yours, I kissed your chin. As my lips touched yours, I saw a grin on your face. I closed mine as I pushed my lips to yours and peered into your eyes one more time. I ran my nails over your warm flesh as I snaked my hands up your waist and around your back.

While our bodies begged for more, we alternated between stroking one other's lips until we ran out of air. I leaned back and absorbed in your presence, committing it to memory. I examined your delicate lips with my thumb, anticipating our next kiss. Your bra was partially covering your breasts as your chest rose and fell. How much has changed since I first saw you made me grin.

Your shirt was on top of mine when I pushed it off of your shoulders and pulled at the sleeves. I gave you a kiss on your bare shoulders and ran my hands lightly up and down your arms to assist you relax. I tried to cup your face in my hands so I could feel your lips once again. I rubbed your bottom lip with my tongue after giving you a few gentle kisses. My bra top was traced by your hands as they moved downward. Your tongue caressed my lips before you withdrew, leaving me wanting more and wanting to return the favor. You got up and extended your hand to me. Will you show me your chamber, or will I have to solve that puzzle on my own?

I grabbed your hand, and you helped me get up. Are you certain about this? Surprising myself, I asked. We've just recently met, yet I already felt like I've known you for a very long time. Nevertheless, I didn't want everything to go too quickly and leave anybody with regrets.

You made a turn and started guiding me down the corridor. Yes, I'm positive. When you started opening doors at random, including the side door going outdoors and into my neighbor's living room, I chuckled. I panicked and slammed the door after checking that it was locked. Are you attempting to have me evicted from the area? I punned. It's very horrible." As the sole lesbian in the neighborhood, I have just terrified my neighbors.

You waved your hand in the air and said, "Oh please," dismissing the idea. If anything, I've simply gotten your HOA charge discounted. I appreciate that, but you owe me a lot.

Is that true? Playing along with you, I questioned.

I'm come to collect, yes ma'am. Where is that bedroom, exactly? If I remember properly, a mirror is located next to the bed.

My face started to flush. Oh, you did recall that, didn't you? As I was guiding you down the corridor to my room at the end, I questioned.

"You made it so I couldn't forget," And as you searched for the mirror, I lighted a few candles. Did you invent it? I fail to notice a mirror.

I pointed and shook my head. "No. The inside of the closet door has it.

"Okay, then, open it." You approached the door while gazing at your reflection after I had opened it. You turned to look at the bed in the mirror behind you and then looked around the room. Are there so many candles in here all the time, or were you hoping for good luck tonight? You whirled around to face the mirror as I approached from behind you.

Do you always have so many inquiries?

You retaliated, "Hey, that's not fair," "I've been the one who has been in the dark all along," she said.

I encircled you in my arms and kissed the back of your neck. "I know. Anything you want to know, ask. We may return downstairs and discuss everything there.

You cocked your head back and leaned towards me, guiding my lips into yours with a hand motion from behind. I softly slid my hands up, gripping your breasts as we intensified our kiss. Your bra was unbuttoned as you reached behind you. I let it fall to the ground as I eased the straps off your shoulders. I ran my fingers over your breasts with both hands while I kissed your shoulder while looking at you in the mirror. You moaned as I massaged your tense nipples with my fingers and palms. I inhaled deeply as I felt the sight of you topless and the low moans you were making make me weak in the knees.

As you looked in the mirror, your gaze alternated between my hands and my eyes. I stopped at the button as I dropped my hands to your jean waist. While I was looking for any hesitancy on your part, you drew me into another passionate kiss. In order to give you time to stop me if you wished, I slowly unbuttoned and unzipped your pants. I broke off the kiss so I could take a breath. I was dizzy from seeing you with your trousers undone and your lovely black panties poking out from beneath your zipper, but I still cracked a big grin.

I stepped forward in front of you and bent down. When I got to the top of your pants, I ran my hands up your thighs. Your legs were dragged all the way to the floor by my fingers as they wrapped around the waistband. I was on my knees in front of you when you kicked them to the side and stepped out of them. I made my way up your thighs while kissing and running my nails up them, making care to avoid your underwear, which I was itching to take off. You were very stunning and alluring.

I was seated on the edge of the bed when you turned away from me. You curved your finger in my direction. Say, "Come over here." As you reached for my pants, I stopped walking and stood in front of you to observe. You unfastened the zipper and button, and I gasped for air. You let your knuckles brush across my clit, and I gasped at the feeling. My jeans were pulled down, and you let them pile up at my feet. I managed to escape from them without averting my gaze from you.

You licked your lips and inquired, "Top or bottom?"

"Wha..what? " I, um, generally...

I choked on my words, and you laughed at me. "What I'm saying is that while you're still wearing your bra and underwear, I'm just halfway nude. Don't get me wrong, I'm loving the eye candy, but eventually the packaging has to be removed. To make us equal, you must decide what to remove. Which comes first?

"Why not make the decision for me?" I squeezed between your stretched-out legs and knelt down to kiss you. I made no attempt to resist as your tongue slithered past my lips to probe even further, making me groan. You dragged me down with you as I gently lowered you back into the bed. Between your legs, my thigh landed and pressed against you. You pulled me harder as you swayed your hips under me, and I could feel your claws cutting into my waist. I forged a route to your breasts by licking and kissing my way down your neck. I gave your right nipple a few soft kisses. You arched your back and buckled your hips in response to my strong tongue flick over the tip of my tongue. I rubbed the nipple against my teeth and tongue while sucking it between my lips. I used my fingers to apply the same torment to your left breast while sensing the movement of your body under mine. I quickly changed sides since I didn't want to overlook any of you. Your right breast, still damp from its previous tongue lashing, was touched by my fingers.

You were laying on the bed in front of me when I felt you go for my bra, so I got up and left. In an effort to be modest, I undid it, covered myself with one arm, and slipped it off with the other. To get a better view, you pulled my arm away as you sat back up. "That's more like it," you said with a smile. I bent my head back and bit my lip as I felt your warm hands on my breasts. You were able to touch me in a way that made my whole body tingle with pleasure. Thoughts of feeling you again consumed all of my thoughts despite how fantastic it felt. I had to kiss you, taste you, and feel you. I wanted to utterly lose myself in you. You made it hard for me to recall that there are other people in the world than you and me. You are the only thing that matters to me when you are on my thoughts.

I dragged your pants down to your ankles because I was unable to contain the yearning that was begging to be satisfied. I gave them one more pull, saying, "Someone's excited," and they eventually fell to the ground. I moved behind you on the bed and kissed you. I was behind you before you knew what was happening. "Get down on your knees," I commanded. "Please?" I added to avoid seeming snarky or demanding.

You knelt down and trembled as you leaned back against me and felt my nipples dance over your back. You drew me in by saying "But I want to see you," and reached behind my head. I moved my hands up to your breasts and kissed your neck. I said, looking in the mirror, "I'm here. I raised my right hand to your side and then to your stomach after waiting for our eyes to connect in the mirror. I lightly drew circles on your stomach.

You inquired, running your fingers over the top of my hand, "What are you doing?"

"I'm enjoying the view," I said. "You are really gorgeous. Do you realize that? I saw as you averted your gaze out of modesty or embarrassment. Your knees widened as a result of my hand dipping farther and going across the top of your inner thigh. It was sufficient to cause you to gaze up once again. I ran my hands up and down the inner of your thighs and kissed your shoulder. Are you certain about this? I asked one final time, my gaze descending below your breasts to my hands moving smoothly over your flawless skin. I glanced in the glass when I didn't hear a reaction and saw you observing my hands, so I stopped moving them. I repeated, "Are you...sure?"

You licked your lips and pulled your hips forward while leaning back into me. You mumbled, "I wouldn't be here if I didn't want this. I just needed to hear that. While my right hand moved ever-closer to where you wanted it, I put my left arm over your front. Your breathing became faster, and my lips were brushed by a racing pulse. "Please. You spat in my ear, "I need to feel your fingertips.

I gently ran the length of my hand against you at first to assure you that I was staying still. My eyes followed yours as I saw you tilting your head forward to see in the mirror. As I applied more pressure while still using my full hand, I saw the look on your face. I was amused by the little groan that came from somewhere deep within your throat as I let my thumb droop over your clit. My fingertips sank lower as they detected your level of arousal. Oh, you were so welcoming and moist. More than any other time in my life, seeing you in the mirror while you watched yourself turned me on. Your dark, lust-filled eyes were hungry and dark. Your bottom lip was drawn in as you clenched your teeth in an effort to be silent.

I slipped my fingers back up over your clit after covering them. You tried to watch as long as you could before your eyelids closed and your eyes rolled back.

I gave you a firm kiss while gently stroking your hair. I said, "Slow down," as you pressed up against my hand. Even though it required more control than I realized I had, I was not going to let this stop so quickly because I wanted it to last. When I saw that you were unwinding and leaning back into me, I increased the pressure of the long, languid strokes. I noticed we weren't in the most comfortable posture when I felt you move. I got out from behind you so you could go back onto the bed and relax.

I grinned, taking the opportunity to view you from this side. You questioned, "What are you smiling at?"

I said, "I can't believe how beautiful you are.

"Yes, I agree."

"It is real. You are flawless. My hands climbed up your thighs. "Your thighs are flawless." I bent forward and slid between your legs, running my thumbs over your nipples. Additionally, "and perfect breasts." I climbed the stairs and gave you another kiss. "I'll bet you taste just as good as you look."

You managed to say, "There's only one way to find out," as I had already started my drop.

I gave your tummy a soft kiss. I glanced up at you, rested my chin, and extended my fingers to the ground. I smiled sarcastically and remarked, "I imagined you a bit more bashful.

You said between gasps, "Sorry to disappoint."

Oh, I didn't say I was dissatisfied. I lowered myself even lower, placing my hands on top of your hips and looping my arms around your thighs. I turned to look at you again, but your eyes were closed and your hands were grasping at anything to save you from being carried away by what you knew was going to happen. Your knees jumped as I kissed the area just above your clit, my chin rubbing on it. I grinned as I glanced up at you and was startled to realize that you were giving me a wide-eyed stare in return. You were tugging at a nipple with one hand as the other was entangled in the sheet and bedcover. You pushed yourself up in an attempt to get close to my lips and tongue. I averted my eyes once again to the space between your swaying thighs and hips as I heard a wretched, "Please," leave your mouth.

You almost got out of bed as I touched the swelling, sensitive area with my tongue. While I had no intention of resisting, I felt a hand on the back of my head pull me closer to you. Your clit was lapped by my tongue repeatedly. I could tell you were loving it nearly as much as I was by the small whimpers and moans I heard. I sank my tongue lower to stroke between your soft lips, flicking it over your clit, and then back down because I wanted to taste more. I like the way you tasted and the sounds made in between your labored gasps as I felt the dampness between my legs sparkle on my own thighs. I couldn't handle the throbbing of my own need that was pleading to be satisfied. It threatened to divert my focus from pleasing you, and I couldn't allow that to happen.

I stuck my tongue as far inside of you as I could while curling the tip. I'll go in and out as your hips follow me. I shifted my hand and arm so that your clit could be teased by my fingers. I could feel your muscles clenching and tightening, but I was still working on you. Your clit was lightly stroked by my lips as I took it softly in my warm tongue. I swiftly back and forth over the small prisoner caught between my lips with the flat of my tongue. You seemed to really like it based on your response. I heard, "Don't stop," just as I was about to quit due to exhaustion. Fuck. Don't ever, ever quit. I used the tip of my tongue to flick against you in various ways as I continued to suck your clit in. Although you didn't complain, I knew it must feel intense—possibly too intense. One hand kept my head steady as your back arched off the bed and you rolled into me. Your thighs toyed with the idea of spreading apart even more or pressing closer to me. "Oh, God. Continue on. Don't stop there, right away.

Your whole body became stiff before turning limp, and you shouted loud enough for the entire neighborhood to hear. When I felt your clit pulsating against my tongue, I gave it a solid kiss and held it there while applying gentle pressure until the little ripples stopped. The delay was well worth it and may have even improved things.

Imagine my disappointment if I woke up during an orgasm only to find out it was all a dream. A fantastic, seductive, and very vivid dream, but just a dream.

And what is that? Do you recall ever having the opportunity to repay the favor? I won't divulge. What do you intend to do to me then? What are you asking that I do to you? Would you want to meet to discuss this?

They continued dating for a few more weeks, making it simpler and more enjoyable each time. They watched a couple movies and an excessive amount of baseball, which Kim found Alison loved. They had a moment at their desks one day during a pause in patient activity.

Hey, how are things going?" the cheery nurse enquired.

She shrugged, "Oh, you know, reconnecting a man's thumb, usual stuff."

Kim chuckled as she turned to face Alison and used a finger to trace her arm. So, last night was fantastic.

Guys, I'm extremely glad for you, but I'm working here, Staci replied, turning to face the audience. The women swiftly gave over the paperwork for their patients. Staci said, "Thanks," sounding plainly exhausted.

That evening had even more intrigue! They made the decision to spend a pleasant evening together. a couple beers, a movie, and dinner. It developed into so much more. During the movie, Kim began to lean against Alison. Her head was resting on Alison's shoulder. A soft hand gently moved up onto her thigh and started tracing up and down while toying with the hem of her skirt.

Kim turned inside, kissing Alison's naked shoulders as the movie began to finish. She let her lips to slowly and softly go closer to her shoulder until they reached her neck. Alison's respiration became a bit deeper. She let her head to fall back, exposing her neck, and her lips to fully relax.

Then Kim straddled her, continuing to kiss Alison's neck and gorgeous lips while she did so. Alison let one hand find her thigh and slipped up to her hip as Kim gradually started to very softly sway her hips. The other settled into a cozy position at her side. Alison's fingers crept beneath Kim's shirt as their desire grew and their tongues danced.

The little woman carefully lowered her top, but Alison had already been seduced too much. Her bra and top were soon torn off of her. When Alison saw Kim's breasts, she stopped, uncertain of what to do with them. Although they looked delectable, they were really unlike to anything she had ever used before. Kim's areolas were somewhat buffed up, and her nipples extended just beyond them. Her nipples were well defined.

Kim went in for a kiss after seeing her apprehension and said, "It's okay, treat them how you like yours played with." Then, while she continued to kiss Alison, she pulled her long blonde hair out of her face and held it over her head in a balled fist. However, Alison pushed her aside and sat up. She started licking Kim's delicate nipples before moving on to the little breasts. When she felt one of them brush up against the edge of her lips, she started kissing all the way around, making sure to tickle their areolas and giving them a little peck with her tongue.

She then started unbuttoning her shit as she made her way up to Kim's lips. As if she were still in high school, Alison's hands were trembling. She was unsure of what to do or anticipate, but Kim made her feel at ease. To remove her bra, Alison thrust her pelvis forward and arched her back. Kim seized the chance to kiss her all the way down her body as she slipped down her slender legs.

Kim slowly gave Alison a side-to-side kiss that extended beyond her belly button. As she moved forward, she increased her pressure. She quickly found herself next to her lover's ample breasts. She started kissing one and rubbing the other. Alison stroked her arms up and down Kim's arm as she began to groan and breathe deeply.

Kim put Alison's nipple in her mouth and used her little tongue to massage it. She first gave it the runaround before progressively starting to fail. Alison whimpered and her hips began to swing in response. As she sucked, Kim felt her tongue sliding across the top of her breast as it moved back and forth between her lips. Kim pushed Alison's skirt down by inserting her deft fingertips inside the waistband.

Alison was staring up at Kim as she glanced up. While anticipating Kim,

Alison licked the corner of her tongue and looked down at her. While maintaining eye contact, Kim lowered herself awkwardly and started kissing Alison's suddenly exposed waist. Her eager, inexperienced lover nearly bucked when Kim kissed the tops of her naked thighs.

Nothing Alison had ever felt before could compare to the sensation of touching such soft, kind, and patient lips. All the guys simply wanted to screw her and yank off her underwear. Kim was in a league of her own. Alison's mound and the tops of her thighs were covered with thin lips. She even offered Alison a playful nibble; when Kim bit into the tender flesh inches from her moist lips, Alison yelped a little and chuckled.

She quickly lost her patience with the mischievous tease. She was anxious and ecstatic, and the suspense was killing her. Her legs were hurting and damp, begging for more. Alison's thighs, which were bound together by the skirt's waist, rubbed her precisely with each movement. She took down her skirt and kissed Kim while holding her hair in one hand and slipping the other down Kim's trousers with the other.

The absence of a penis felt so strange. Of course, but it was also strangely familiar. Alison was less svelte than Kim. Her lips shrank and became closer to her torso. Kim had longer, more prominent labia, which was another distinction. When Alison ran her fingers through them, they were very velvety. She started rapidly rubbing Kim and kissed her more. Kim quickly transitioned from kissing to rocking into her hand and groaning into her lips. "Like that baby, exactly."

Alison was ecstatic and very sensual when she heard Kim call her baby. She poked her middle finger inside of Kim's constricted body and felt how wet Kim was. She took hold of Alison's finger and muttered, "another," into her ear before starting to bite her neck. Kim played some of her own as a second finger slipped in between her lips.

Alison's very delicate and big lips were seen when Kim pulled back the lace undergarments. Then, Alison reclined back and relaxed her body's breathing. Kim carefully lowered herself to the ground while letting her underwear drop back over her. She gave her beau a chest kiss before moving on to her belly. Then Alison widened her legs and let her ass slip forward.

Kim began by kissing the tops of her thighs and her naval before moving on to her underwear. She lowered herself till her head was directly in between Alison's large thighs. The lace did nothing to protect Alison's overexcited body as lips discovered her lips. Kim placed her arms over those gorgeous thighs while shifting her knees back slightly on the carpet. Kim would sometimes tear herself away from burying her face in Alison's underwear to kiss and even nibble at her thighs.

Alison could no longer stand it as Kim continued to kiss her. Kim rubbed up to her, and she felt every millimeter of feeling. It was excruciating as the minutes passed and the lace gathered wet. Alison froze as Kim's fingers started circling her hips. That moist cover was removed when fingers caught the lace.

When Alison felt a strong pull, she nearly fell off the sofa since she was completely vertical except for her head. Kim clutched the back of her neck as she continued to look into those blue eyes. She brought their tongues together for deeper kissing, pushing her hips into Alison's tender flower.

Kim then pulled her boyfriend down one more while she was still shaking. She reclined and saw a thin, shimmering stream of liquid extending from her waist to the ground. You wicked little child, she said as she glanced up with the most cunning expression on her face.

Alison's head dipped and her eyes started to roll back into her head as Kim crept up to her crotch. Alison's lips were traced by Kim's deftly shaped tongue, which had become a solid point. One lip down, her wetness encircled, and the other lip up. She started off softly kissing, barely touching, just enough to let every nerve know she was there but not enough to irritate. She started kissing gradually harder and harder.

Alison's gushing sex was softly touched by her tongue, which slowly gathered the lovely nectar and massaged it up to her clit.

Her tiny pearl had expanded and became exceedingly sensitive from all the teasing and excitement. As her body was being aroused, Alison groaned. She then grabbed Kim's hair and peered down to see a sneaky little grin appear on her face.

Then, Kim started licking all over, trying to cover as much of her mouth as she could. All of Alison's anxiety dissipated as the tightness between her legs as she enjoyed it. Alison writhed as the powerful tongue gradually made its way inside of her. She continued to press Kim's head towards her while squeezing her own nipples. As more people saw her clit, the tension increased. As Kim went on, the swelling of ecstasy grew.

Alison raised herself on her elbows so she could see the work of this young, enchanting lady. She concentrated on Alison's clit by moving her tongue over it. She started out gently before picking up speed in a steady pattern. Her eyes pleaded and were thrilled with Kim as her lips hung wide. Even a little saliva leaked from her lips. Kim stood up after seeing this, licked it, and gave her a kiss. Alison had never previously thought that her own pussy tasted wonderful after the boys had done, but Kim's tongue made Alison think otherwise.

Kim returned to her work after showing off by dripping a little saliva over the delicate pearl. It made her irrational. Kim put her lips over that little delight buzzer and started licking once again. As the pace and pressure increased, her hips began to sway in anticipation of the blow. Alison's hips lifted onto Kim's tongue as she shook her body to keep it there. It was too much in less than a minute; the stress sent waves through her pussy. She began to feel tingles between her legs, and in the excitement, her nipples even rose.

Now was so near to that excruciatingly close climax. The speed at which Kim's tongue was moving increased pressure as the finale approached. Kim was forced into Alison's pussy as Alison felt the sensations explode. She collapsed to the ground, her knees locking tightly around Kim's head, and she blew out like a bomb.

She simultaneously stumbled and yelled, "Oh...God." At that point, Kim began to flick her tongue. Alison becomes uncomfortable and pulls the woman away. Her body sent a wave out, soaking the cushion under her in the process. As she reentered the world and started to giggle, Alison panted. With her tongue,

Kim took a little amount of that fluid and spilled it over Alison's huge breasts. It settled in the crevices of her arms after sliding down her nipples and the sides of her breasts.

Kim re-ascended on top of her and positioned herself across her hips. Alison stood back up and sat down. That was incredible, she gushed. Kim questioned, "Have you ever done that before?" Alison yelled, "No," while grinning. As soon as she stopped crying, they continued kissing and discussed it. Alison was eager for their next meeting since she was so at ease with Kim.

Kim placed herself onto Alison's face and whispered with a sly grin, "Good, because it's my turn now." Her sly eyes flared as she did so. Alison started kissing, and soon the groaning resumed.

Did she even intend to attend? Max thought he was such a moron. She was unable to explain what took place in those restrooms, but something did. Everyone was astonished, but she refrained from pressing Frances since she felt bad for her and wanted to know what had occurred, but she didn't want to risk offending her. The girl would feel intimidated if she was pushed. She was aware of it. She would respond that way. Was it proper for her to keep what occurred quiet? Max began to create all of those terrifying scenarios, some of which saw her fired for absurd reasons. She brushed these ideas aside. She decided to focus on extracting as much information as she could from Frances for the time being. She had a sinking feeling that she should keep the entire thing a secret until she was certain that risking more damage to Frances' academic record would be worthwhile. It wasn't always wise to act honestly.

When Max heard a faint knock, the door cracked open just a little. The instructor got the impression from Frances' confident demeanor that she was about to confess to some kind of crime as she entered the room. Frances snatched up a chair and began dragging it up to the woman's desk. "The lass is a girl I used to have a thing with," she said. She took issue with the fact that I had an extramarital relationship. We were never official-" She dropped her weight into the chair and crossed her legs. "-at least not in my eyes, and yes, I was driving fast this afternoon."

The lady merely sat there with her mouth open and a red pen still in her hand, as if she had caught Max off guard. Frances offered the lady a shy grin while tucking a lock of her black hair behind her ear. Max reciprocated the gesture.

I'm amazed you actually showed up, she murmured.

"I really appreciated the way you spoke to me today…" Frances started to sound slightly unsure. I need assistance, but I really want to smoke. Can we get out of here?"

The professor shrugged. She returned the girl's gaze, saying, "Yeah sure." "You smoke?" That explained the raspy voice.

Frances guffawed. "Social smoker by age 15, ten to fifteen cigarettes per day by age 18. I'd think it's a very typical trend.

"Let me just pack up, and then we can go outside and give ourselves lung cancer."

Frances lit her Benson and Hedges Gold as Max watched. She fought the wind for a little while before covering the cigarette with her hands.

The girl breathed out, "Thanks. To be honest, you don't seem to be the smoking kind.

They were moving toward the nearest park when Max laughed. For six o'clock, it was quite quiet. Darkness was setting in. "What does a smoker even look like?" she asked rhetorically whilst taking a drag of her own cigarette. She loved the gross, musky smell of them.

Frances knew better than to answer. "Do you think I can get into uni?" She seemed worried. "As in, get any offers. I don't know how to sell myself in the application."

We can address it. Do you know the courses in which you are most interested?

The girl spoke quickly and said, "Creative Writing." I said, "Have you read my poem yet?"

Max instantly had a recollection and felt a little awkward. She was covering her drug use while chatting about her gorgeous sensual poetry that had the term "orgasm" in a park with a pupil. She began to feel a little bit predatory as she saw the eighteen-year-old smoking a cigarette with large, kissable red lips while wearing a huge green coat and a grey beanie.

Indeed, I did.

Frances gave her a hopeful glance, but her face immediately turned amused. She halted her progress. "Mrs. Cordona, are you all right?"

Max inhaled deeply and shrugged off his apprehension. "Uh, sure, I'm good. By the way, it's Max. Yes, I read it. I'm not surprised you think creative writing is for you since it was pretty fantastic. However, they were designed to remain unidentified. That's probably my fault. She swiftly said, "I should have informed you.

After a brief attempt to read her, Frances gave up and sat down on the closest bench to light up another cigarette. Max's senses were heightened by the cozy lighting.

"I believed I might have become. I didn't like the thought of you or anybody else perhaps associating the incorrect poetry with me and developing an inaccurate impression of who I am. As she sat next to the instructor, she spoke gently while keeping an eye on her. The black-haired girl thought it was beautiful how Max struggled to overcome her attraction to the female. Hope it's okay with you.

Max nodded, entirely forgetting what she had been considering up until that point. The rejection of anonymity is intriguing. Frances either has a high self-esteem when it comes to writing or she worries a lot about what other people think of her. What one is it? she questioned.

Before she could stop herself, it was already too late. She said out of the blue, "Why do you take drugs?"

Frances straightened her spine as the phrase instantly sent her into a panicked state. After a little while, she turned to face the instructor with a new, more relaxed look. Why do you want to kiss me, exactly? mostly because people desire to feel and accomplish things. It's not difficult. Max was glad that the girl wasn't angry at her for asking when she shrugged, but the teacher's stomach fell when the word "kiss" struck her. The girl was now quite near to her face, so she turned to look at her. Max was afraid to move. Although the logical half of her mind wanted Frances to go, the bulk of her body and mind yearned for interaction. Her cigarette breath was now detectable to her. After glancing at

Max's lips, Frances turned to face her directly.

She really wanted to get out of this predicament, but Frances, who had enormous hair, red lips, and a magnificent green coat, simply stood up and walked away, holding her unfinished cigarette in her left hand.

Max narrowly avoided colliding with anything or anybody while driving home. Her brain felt like it was about to blow up. In most cases, when there is mutual attraction—and Max was certain that there was—you simply get over it and get on with your life, but not in this case. Despite the fact that they shouldn't have been there in the first place, Frances managed to encircle Max without even trying.

The instructor removed her phone from her pocket and put her bag on the couch. Thankfully, a couple of the females she had been seeing were out tonight as she called a few numbers to see if any of them were available. To calm herself down, she crossed the living room, went into the kitchen, and poured a shot of vodka for herself. drinking after school. Max retrieved her phone and put it up to her ear.

Hey fam, feared you passed away in class or something," crooned a happy voice.

"Hey Sam," the instructor said. "Are you currently busy? I need to chat because I'm so screwed up and need to vent. I was hoping for a boost tonight since I was also going to see Kelsey.

"The doctor? She was told by her closest buddy of over 13 years, "Thought you weren't into her. "Sure, I'll be over in twenty, hang in there."

I bid you a hearty "cheers, mate."

The other lady ended the call with, "See you soon, knobhead."

With Sam, twenty minutes normally equated to forty, and it was already eight o'clock so the instructor made the decision to begin preparing.

By the time Sam got to Max's home, the instructor had changed her mind a million times, going from telling Sam the truth to not telling Sam the truth. Even though she knew Sam would keep the secret secure, speaking it out would make it true, and Max was most afraid of that. She never even contemplated the prospect that she would fall head over heels for one of her pupils and go so far as to stand vigil over her.

The best buddy inquired as he filled the kettle, "So what's this thing you wanna get off your chest, man?" She looked in the cabinet for coffee. Did you deceive your mother once more?

Max sipped from her vodka and coke while seated at one of the kitchen countertops. Sam saw where this was headed and stared at the instructor in surprise when the teacher said, "There is this one student."

"I accidentally discovered that she was having an affair and chose not to disclose it. I'm obsessed with how drawn to her I am. Sighing, Max. She explicitly said today that she is aware of and feels the same way.

"You idiot," Sam said as she poured hot water into her cup. The kettle then shut off. "Is she legal?"

Max gave the other lady a middle finger while rolling her eyes.

"If someone finds out, you might lose your job, and it might be difficult for you to find a new one with that on your record." The best buddy seemed to be reflecting. But not against the law. I'm not sure, family. depends on how much you like your work and if you think it's worth it to spend all this time with one female. You keep hearing stories about these adolescents acting out of control and threatening you. It may get ugly.

The professor nodded. "True." She groaned. I'm going to attempt to let it go.

Sam glowed. "And Kelsey... is a distraction," she said. Her closest friend's sentence was completed by Max.

You really are a dickhead, she chuckled. When was that? It's almost ten; should I give you a ride?

Matt nodded.

I was playing squash the other day because I wanted to be active and healthy, and I also like sports where I can compete and use my hands. It's only that when I approached 35, I hadn't yet discovered any restrictions and had always felt unstoppable—that is, until I suddenly began to have severe discomfort in my neck and down my right leg. I first believed that it would just go away on its own, but it quickly became clear that I would need to take action. I've always assumed that I'm immune to the illnesses that others complain about having, but maybe I was mistaken.

I made the decision to see my doctor, and now I'm sitting here waiting for the findings. He enters the room with the air of someone who has nothing on his mind. He takes a seat and turns to face me with a more serious expression. "I think you could have strained a muscle in your shoulder, back, or leg. Given how difficult it is to treat, I believe the only option will be to take painkillers to dull the discomfort. I asked him if there was anything else I could do or if there was an alternative therapy that might assist me since the idea of being dependent on painkillers did not really appeal to me.

I interrupted him mid-sentence and asked him what she did and if it might be useful for me. He sat there thinking for what seemed like an eternity, "I personally think alternative therapy is a lot of mumbo jumbo even though my wife practices it." Well, she does Swedish massage and also does reflexology so if you want to contact her here this is her number but I think the painkillers are the best option. I thanked him for his support and informed him that I would try painkillers and speak with his wife. That evening, the agony became intolerable, so I called her and made plans to talk with her the next day about what may be able to assist.

When I went to the reception that morning at the clinic where she worked, a very harsh elderly lady welcomed me and instructed me to sit down until she called Tina to come down and take me upstairs. I had the impression that I was in a hospital, albeit maybe things were different upstairs. The receptionist called while I was still waiting and instructed me to go up the stairs to door number 30. I pulled my brown hair behind my head and pulled it into a ponytail as I went down the hallway in my 5 foot, 2-inch frame. Since we were simply having a conversation, I wasn't wearing any makeup. Anyway, many had told me I was attractive without wearing makeup since I exercised so much, but in my heart of hearts, I wasn't sure if this was true.

When I eventually made it to the door, it was off to the side and at the end of the corridor. When I knocked on the door, a lady with really long, black, curly hair who was dressed in a white massage outfit that complemented her hair so well answered. She seemed extremely welcoming, and I immediately relaxed. She motioned for me to enter before lighting some incense and touching some wind chimes' bells.

"When I informed your husband about the discomfort I was experiencing, he said you may be able to assist me. I am aware that I may take painkillers for it, but I truly do not want to depend on drugs. Your husband suggested that I chat with you about if you have any treatments that would assist with the severe pain in my shoulders and legs. She also had extremely white skin that looked like snow, which made her long, black hair appear even darker. I saw she had very red cherry lips, which made me envious since I did not have the same feature myself. She looks like she's in her mid-40s, but she also has a young, innocent aspect to her face, and as she sat down, I got the impression that she would be helpful and kind.

First of all, my name is Tina. Would you want to take a stroll in the garden across the street because it's beautiful outside and this room is somewhat formal? She walked with such a peaceful stride and looked to be a really relaxed person, so even though it was unexpected, I was pleased to go for a walk since I was now not exercising at all since my injury had gotten me. I assume my spouse has already informed you that he believes all of my alternative treatments are crap, Kelly? I hope it's OK if I use your first name. I had to confess that I did not anticipate this, but she did assist in making me feel at ease. I want you to feel at ease and think of me as a wonderful friend starting today.

"My husband's issue is that he doesn't understand how the body can heal itself or how to experience the pleasure that heals," I said. When she stated that, I was reflecting on how I had not had any sexual activity with my own spouse for a while, and that the only sexual activity I had experienced was tennis, which I was no longer able to play. I can assure you, Kelly, that you won't need the painkillers your doctor has prescribed if you become friends with me and accept my assistance. She said that, and hearing that made me so thrilled to have met her.

I want Kelly to know that I've been doing this for ten years and that I've learned a variety of ways. I promise that one of them will help you get some relief from the agony you're experiencing right now. She was about 3 inches taller than I was, and as we walked, I could see that she had a fantastic figure. I had not noticed this at first, but as we continued walking, I could see that she was very toned. "I tell you Kelly this is the only exercise that I do, and I feel great. No calorie counting just walking, pure healthy foods," she said.

Kelly, enough about me. Please explain your issue and the source of your suffering. I informed her that it affected both my shoulders and my legs and that I had never previously explored any alternative treatments. I also admitted to her that I was unsure of what to anticipate and if I would feel at ease. She gave me an encouraging smile as she assured me, "I'll take care of you Kelly, so you don't need to worry."

"What we can do is have you come here on Friday night about 7 o'clock when you get off work.I felt that this was a great idea since I did not enjoy sitting at reception and having other people know my business. The clinic is so peaceful at that hour because most people had left for the day.Additionally, Kelly, you are free to utilize the nice, warm showers when you arrive or after our treatment if you so like.

That evening, I made the decision to research Tina online to learn more about her. Her website, which provided evaluations of persons in the holistic field, was among the top few results. As I read the reviews, I saw that the bulk of them were written by women, and they were all quite positive and said she had a beautiful approach that had really benefited them. One young Indian woman said that Tina gave her the finest massage of her life and focused on the places that she desired.

Knowing that other ladies had left positive evaluations after seeing her helped me feel much more at ease and prevented me from continuing to use painkillers. As I relaxed and took in the evening, I started to consider if going to see Tina may not be a terrible idea. Although I knew nothing about her, it seemed legitimate enough. She seemed to be a pleasant woman with a good mood.

When I awoke the morning of my appointment with Tina, I checked my answering machine. There, I found a message from Tina explaining that there had been a mix-up and that she could now only do 30 to 40 minutes of therapy. She also offered to work on my shoulders for 30 minutes if I was still okay with that, saying that this would be a good start before scheduling another appointment. She was right, and I phoned her back to tell her that I agreed with her and would see her later. Many of my coworkers told me it was all in my brain and that I was simply being too cautious? Only after talking to Tina did I finally find someone who was ready to try and assist me while still being cordial with me.

I made the decision that morning to wear a wonderful, seductive pink bra to work with my white shirt just because I knew Mark, who I was teaching how to do my job, was always glancing at me. I reasoned that if the young man was going to continue staring at me in that manner, I should once in a while indulge in a little evilness and tease him by leaving a button undone. I needed to feel loved, and doing this was my own way to get through the day by having a little dangerous fun.

I had a 7 o'clock appointment with Tina, but since I was in a protracted meeting with my boss and coworkers and it was now past 6 o'clock, I knew I would not be able to get home in time to change. Once the allotted 30 minutes had passed, I ran to my vehicle and left to see Tina.

When I got at the clinic, there were no vehicles at all and it seemed that no one was inside, exactly as she had warned me. The gruff receptionist was not present when I arrived; instead, Tina was waiting in the waiting area and was prepared to welcome me. She wore bright red lipstick and her hair seemed much longer and wavier than the day before as I moved closer to her. She was also sporting a different uniform than the one she had on the previous occasion; this one was pink and revealed more of her lower neckline as well as hints of her bra. She seemed to be getting ready to go, so I wondered whether she did this often for appointments. But then I realized that she did like dressing up and taking care of herself. She did seem stunning.

Once again seeing how fantastic she looked, I thought to myself that if she could ease my pain, I would go to the gym as often as I could to obtain a body like hers as we ascended the stairs with her leading the way.

"All right Kelly, what we're going to do today is give you a shoulder and neck massage, and I think I might be able to help you with that pain a little bit." To properly work on your shoulders, I'll need you to remove your blouse. I instantly realized that I was donning an extremely exposing and seductive bra at that same time, but it was too late and I couldn't simply go. She instructed me to relax by sitting down on a chair, but as I did so, I felt very exposed. It was also extremely strange to be sitting in a quiet room wearing a seductive bra.

After combining some oils, she turned around and her face revealed disbelief at what I was wearing before telling me I looked fantastic. She approached me carefully after that and said she would start massaging some oil into my neck and shoulders. As she stepped behind me and flung my hair off of my neck, she said, "Just relax, just breathe, and enjoy the warm air and the sound of nature all around you." I made an effort to do just that, but given my health at the time, it was challenging.

I first recoiled when she touched my shoulders, but eventually I fell into it and let her massage her hands into the area of pain that was bothering me the most. She was able to massage a smaller region, but she was unable to completely relieve the discomfort. Almost enough for me to beg her to stop as her fingers rubbed across my shoulders, but I didn't. She continued, and as she massaged into my shoulder, I felt the fabric and buttons of her uniform moving closer to my back. This, along with the way her hands were working, caused a really pleasant chill to travel down my spine.

After a while, I felt myself almost drifting off, and when I finally woke up from my reverie, I could feel air on my neck because she was now so close to it and massaging the front of it in a way I had never experienced before. I sighed deeply, but I was also relieved to have met this woman because she is always going to be of assistance to me. I don't know how long we were in the room, but it felt like an eternity, and then I saw the time and realized we had to go shortly. She appeared to be having a great time assisting me and was clearly very focused on what she was doing; at this point, she was shockingly close to my neck, although she did admit to use a variety of methods. She stopped what she was doing gradually and made gentle gestures before telling me it was finished and getting my reaction. I immediately told her it was amazing, and she grinned back and said, "Kelly, that was just 30 minutes. Imagine when we have an hour."

She instructed me to drink water and to take it easy as I stood up, my breasts showing through my bra. She was sometimes glancing at my bra as she was chatting, but I suppose it was difficult to ignore since it stuck out so much.

"Tina Can I schedule an hour-long meeting with you anytime despite the fact that I am aware of your constant busyness and large clientele? If having a little period of relaxation and pleasure feels like this, I'm prepared to try your approaches.

"I'll call you Kelly when I get home and check my calendar since I've been very busy with clients recently, but I'm certain we can fit you in soon. We may schedule a time when it is quiet again and talk over the phone about what your next course of therapy will be. It was sound counsel, and I realized that I wanted to relive this particular moment between us, so I told her, "That suits me well." I was so light after leaving her clinic and had no discomfort at all.

Emma found herself in front of Lily's home in a tiny black dress for the second time in two days, causing Lily to lust for her.

All she knew was that she wanted to do what Lily desired, but she had no idea why.

When the doorbell rang, nobody answered it. After waiting for five minutes, Emma heard nothing from the door's other side.

When Emma finally tested the door, she discovered that it was unlocked.

Emma entered the room in the dark.

The only source of illumination in the living room was the light that entered via the windows in the kitchen and living area; otherwise, the space was completely dark.

"Lily?" Emma yelled.

Nobody responded.

Before being pulled back by an arm around her neck and having a handkerchief placed to her nose, all she heard was the gentle sound of bare feet tapping on the carpet.

***

Emma was positioned against the wall, facing a bed, with her feet and arms restrained.

When Emma opened her eyes, Lily was sitting cross-legged on that bed, grinning and looking at her with a glint in her eye.

Lily said, "up up.

What the eff? Why are you acting like a maniac? Emma growled, attempting to free her arms and legs from the nylon ropes shackling them.

"I can tell that you dressed well for me. I really like your outfit. I can obviously see your cleavage in that outfit, and trust me, it looks wonderful!"

Emma gave up and closed her eyes after realizing it was pointless to fight the ropes.

"Lily, why are you acting like this? What do you desire?

"Do you realize what the one thing is that control freaks like you despise? It's getting out of hand. However, they detest another thing even more than losing control. Do you recognize that? As

Lily sprang out of bed and moved near Emma, she asked.

"I don't know," Emma said in response.

After giving Emma a kiss, Lily approached the blonde and dropped down on her knees in front of her. "It is losing domination of the thing they own, to someone else," Lily remarked.

What actions do you have in mind, Lily? Don't you realize how childish you are acting? Nothing will be resolved by tying me up.

"I know. Before I give you the main course, officer, I'll tie you up. Come on in, dear, I want you to meet someone very important right now, Emma said as she rose up.

Emma saw the bedroom door opening before seeing a lady enter.

With brilliant red hair, emerald eyes, and a curvy body that indicated she worked out often, the lady was quite attractive. She approached Lily as she arrived and immediately embraced her in a close hug. She was around Lily's age.

When the passionate kissing between the two females ended, Lily turned to Emma and gave her a bear embrace before introducing herself as Tracy. I credit her for making me adore being a slave. She was also a wonderful mistress to me. She forced me to act in ways toward her that both hurt and made me happy.

You were a wonderful slave, too. When you finally showed up at my door after all these years, I was astonished. I assumed you had given up the way of life permanently.

I had, in fact. However, this woman's presence brought those emotions back, and guess what, Mistress? She doesn't even want to hire me as her slave. In an effort to make her wake up to her true potential as an alpha and take control of what is rightfully hers, I had to draw you away from your dull marriage in order to dominate me once again.

Do you honestly believe this will succeed? Emma questioned as she turned her gaze from Tracy to Lily and back to Tracy.

"Any hopeless sex-deprived maniac can try!" Lily swung Tracy around to face her and whispered, Should we begin right now, my Mistress?

"Yes! Remove all of the clothing off your body and bring the collar and leash. I haven't seen those wonderful legs or those lovely tits of yours in years. But hold on, let me see whether you still scream in that same adorable way that you used to in college," remarked Tracy, grabbing Lily by the hair and yanking her firmly in her direction before biting down on her lip to make her scream in the prettiest manner imaginable.

"Oh, you sure do! Now go collect the supplies.

Emma stared in awe at what was taking place in front of her, and while she struggled to accept it, jealously was already beginning to grip her.

Lily crawled on all fours toward Tracy, who was also just wearing her underwear, while holding the leash and collar in her teeth.

Tracy placed the collar around Lily's neck, fastened the leash to the collar, and gave a little pull. Lily's head jerked forward, causing Tracy to exhale and giggle.

Emma experienced the pain once again along with a tingling in her pussy.

She briefly thought of forcing Lily to crawl on all fours while she held the leash, and for that split second, she thought she was in paradise.

"You look amazing in this. similar like a small bitch in the heat. So she is the lady who made you feel so hopeless that you contacted me? What makes her so unique? She does have a really attractive appearance and reminds me of Shakira, but apart from that, she doesn't strike me as a dominatrix. Look at her pouting in the corner as she is restrained. Tracy looked straight at Emma as she added, "A dominatrix can never be tied up. " She then gave the leash another pull, this time more forcefully.

"Come, Lily, sample the lady of your dreams. Who knows if or when you'll have another chance to taste her. Get here, bitch.

Lily followed Tracy as she brought her to the spot where Emma was impaled on the wall.

Say, "Suck her toes."

Emma's heels were quickly taken off by Lily, who then quickly knelt down to grab Emma's toe in her mouth.

Lily closed her eyes as she licked on her toe in pure enjoyment.

Emma too experienced pleasure, but she was unable to stop it.

That's all I need. Lily hesitantly released go of Emma's toe and put Tracy's in her mouth when Tracy instructed, "Now suck on my toe."

Who has superior taste? Which toe do you like sucking the most?

Lily continued to suck on Tracy's toe without responding.

"Whore, I questioned you."

The toe. Yes, Mistress, your toe. I can suck it for hours on end. It doesn't even need to be cleaned for me.

Tracy told Lily, "Good, now come here," and dragged her to the bed.

Tracy maintained one leg on the edge of the bed and the other firmly on the floor as she stood next to the bed.

Between my legs, please. Please position yourself exactly below my pussy. Yes, I'll get hold of those straight, silky black hair, exactly like that tiny slut. Oh, they are so wonderful. Kiss my pussy now.

Lily took hold of Tracy's leg that was still on the ground and slid her face between Tracy's thighs, kissing and sucking Tracy's pussy lips all the way down.

Lily's head was pushed away from her pussy by Tracy, who then turned to face her slave.

What had I requested of you?

Say, "Kiss your pussy."

The question "And what did you do?"

It was "kissed."

Did you just give it a kiss?

"No, Mistress, I also licked it. But I was unable to resist. I didn't really like it the last time I was confined to this position, with a lady towering above me and my face buried in her crotch. Lily remarked in a very sweet, adorable voice, "But with you, I simply couldn't contain myself. She then glanced straight at Emma, who just rolled her eyes.

I could care less. You will need to pay a price for this. Observe me. Continue gazing at my eyes. Your gorgeous eyes are making my pussy so moist, fuck. Tracy spat on Lily's kohl-lined eyes, dripping saliva down her lashes, and remarked, "It's a shame I'll have to do this.

"I was mistaken. With my spit all over them, your eyes seem even more lovely.

You spat on her as a kind of discipline? You must be a novice," sneered Emma.

Would you want to respond to what the lady whose pussy you detested eating just said?

Lily picked up some of Tracy's spit from her eyes, put it on her tongue, and then swallowed it, saying, "I would like to reply by doing this."

"Lily, I am aware of what you are doing. You want for me to feel envious. You want me to demonstrate how to do it to this newbie. Simply say it, and I'll carry it out.

Oh, I had said it many times that evening. It's too late now. I'm having too much fun gratifying my new mistress to really care about you. Then, Mistress, may I please re-insert my face into your pussy? "Yes, you may, but only because I liked your response to that fake dominatrix."

Lilu dove back between Tracy's legs and started licking her pussy with long, passionate licks while making sure Emma had a good view of the way her tongue rolled over Tracy's swollen pussy lips, the way her lips brushed her clit, the way her hands were squeezing Tracy's ass, and the way Tracy was gently stroking Lily's hair as if she were not only her slave but also her lover.

Although Emma had previously developed a jealous streak due to Tracy's dominance and severe treatment of Lily, it was the love and passion in the events playing out in front of her that eventually convinced her to give in.

Emma commanded Lily to come and untie her.

Lily ignored him, blissfully closing her eyes as she continued to kiss Tracy's pussy.

"Lily!" Louder, "Come here and untie me immediately, you filthy, cunning slut," Emma commanded. Your superior has given you this directive. Untie me so I may have true pleasure, please. Come here to find out what it's like to be a true alpha's obedient slave! I am a lady who has murdered people and forced billionaire's spouses to surrender to me. Even Hailey, the precinct chief, has been raped to death by me. Now come here and spend time with a lady who will cause you to cry both happy and painful tears. COME!" Emma yelled and violently wrenched her wrists apart from one another, causing the rope to break and release her hands from all shackles.

Lily grinned and remarked, "Looks like the alpha has finally awakened."

What do you want to do now, Lily? Emma grinned back and said. I am in charge here and might go at any time.

Then, what would you do? Continue to serve...her? Tracy was the target of Emma's pointing.

"I would hate for you to go straight away. I want you to come.

Emma responded, her voice frigid and her face expressionless, "Then crawl out from under her legs, remove your leash and collar, and come to me."

Lily moved quickly, unhooking the collar and tossing the leash aside before crawling over to Emma, who was now standing upright and grinning at Lily while wearing a short, tight dress.

Is this the end? I had anticipated that it would need much more! I was unable to enjoy myself. Tracy grumbled while keeping one leg on the bed.

Tracy, do you want to have fun? Then you will have to do something you have never done before," Emma remarked, "What?"

"Honey, you will also have to become my slave. In this space, there can only be one dominatrix, and that is me. Have we not made that quite obvious, Lily?"

Lily remained silent but rose to her knees, resting her face between Emma's thighs as she moaned, purring like a kitten.

'I can't do that. A dominatrix, I am. Dominance is in my blood.

"Tracy, come here."

Emma groaned, marched towards Tracy, and caught up to her before she could respond with "I won't."

Tracy was pushed against the wall by Emma, who then aggressively and passionately started making out with her while holding the back of her head.

Tracy attempted to get away from Emma, but she was helpless against the seasoned policewoman. Within seconds, Tracy started to melt into the kiss and started reacting by putting Emma's tongue in her mouth and sucking on it like a penis.

As Tracy whimpered in agony, Emma grabbed her behind and gave her a severe spanking.

Smack.

Smack.

Smack.

Tracy screamed at the third one because it was the toughest. The redhair hugged Emma and started to rub Emma's pussy against her thighs, but she wouldn't stop sucking on her tongue.

Tracy was enjoying himself, but soon enough Emma stepped aside and said, "On your knees, right now."

Tracy complied with instructions.

"Now get on your knees and crawl over to Lily."

"Yes," Tracy said.

"Yes, but who?"

"Yes," "Mistress?"

I'm a policewoman, so no. You may address me as "officer." Emma pointed at Lily and shouted, "And you too, you dirty slut.

Lily mumbled, "Yes, Officer."

The two sat on their knees, nude and obedient, awaiting commands from their new mistress. Tracy soon joined Lily.

"Lily, you said you loved my ass, right?"

"Yes, Officer, ever since I saw it, I've been yearning over it. I haven't seen a better ass in a long.

"Great. Soon enough, you will have a decent taste of it, said Emma, who moved in between Lily and Tracy so that Tracy was facing Emma's crotch and Lily was standing behind her with her face only centimeters from Emma's ass.

With Lily pressing her face against Emma's ass, the hem of Emma's dress hitched up, her eyes closed, and her hands massaging Emma's legs, Lily caught Emma's attention as she stood between her kneeling slaves.

"It seems that Lily finally achieved her goals. But keep in mind that once you become my slave, there is no way out—even if you one day decide that this is not what you desire. You cannot just disappear as you did with Tracy. Tracy is not me. Do you comprehend that?

Officer, I agree. I doubt I'll ever be able to leave you. I am now yours. Even my boyfriend was left behind for you.

"Yes, I am aware. And I was quite amazed by that. And at this point, your companion here, this stunning redhead, will join you in receiving your prize. I enjoy her. She herself is quite attractive. She could also like being a submissive, in my opinion. Will you? Emma questioned, holding Tracy by the chin and forcing her to look up.

"Officer, I believe I will."

Naturally, you will. They all do. Let me simply grip both of your heads and shove them between my knees," Emma replied, opening her legs somewhat wider. She then forced Tracy's face against her pussy and smacked Lily's face into her ass, holding their backs of heads with the power that only she had.

The girls were aware of their obligations. When Lily saw Tracy working her tongue into Emma's pussy, she lost her mind and spread Emma's butt cheeks before sticking her tongue right into Emma's butthole and tongue-fucking Emma's ass while yelling furiously.

"Oh my god fuck yeah! Please clean my behind, Lily. Didn't you desire it, though? Fuck! Until I am unable to stand any longer, I am not letting your face leave my behind. The same is true for you, redhead.

Emma kept her promise. She did not give her slaves even a little moment of rest, keeping their heads mashed on her pussy and ass.

As if their lives depended on it, the two girls gasped, choked, groaned, licked, and damaged their knees, but they persisted in making love to their new mistress, and as far as Lily and Emma were concerned, they now knew their patrols would be considerably more interesting going forward.

***

a year later

Late in the afternoon, when traffic was at its worst, Emma and Lily were eager to get out of the city's bustle and onto the freeway.

"How far is this location from the city?" Once their automobile had avoided the jam and was speeding down the freeway, they asked Lily.

"At least one hour's drive away. You would anticipate ranches to be there, wouldn't you? Richard held his prisoners imprisoned outside the city, where no one can see what you are doing.

"The poor girls must have gone through so much; I can't even begin to understand. You're imprisoned in a ranch's basement and unsure of when you'll be taken away as a sex worker by a buyer. Now, everything makes perfect sense. Because Jacob was also a customer, he was unable to take action against Richard, leaving those unfortunate dancers to take the brunt of his wrath.

"I just hope the FBI agents did a good job gathering all the evidence," she said. I don't want to enter that area and instruct the FBI on how to carry out its duties.

But I have no doubt that you'll still discover something that those men would have overlooked. As the golden rays of the setting sun fell on the cheeks of the two policewomen, Lily praised Emma, "You are simply so brilliant.

"Is this a compliment from my pet or a coworker?"

"Both," a beaming Lily said.

"Oh! Stop grinning like that! You are aware of how cute I think you are when you grin like that.

"I'm unable to stop. Just look at my gorgeous face.

"Well, I'd like to have this cute face suck on my tits for a bit. Do you believe you can do that?

Is this a directive from my queen or a request from a colleague?

A directive from your queen.

Lily stood up from her chair and sat across Emma's lap, facing Emma. "In that case, this slave cannot say no," Lily remarked.

Lily kissed Emma's cleavage, pressed her face against Emma's breast, undid her police shirt, and sucked her nipple in her mouth while Emma giggled.

No matter how much you suck on my tits, I'll always find it enjoyable.

Lily said, "And I don't think I can ever get tired of taking it in my mouth," as their automobile drove down the highway into the setting sun.

It's over.

The bedroom, which had only enough space for a bed, a tiny cabinet, and a table without any chairs, was where I was seated by myself.

My heart was pounding, and my hands were shaking.

After Mia had orgasmed, and before Lucy could stop giggling uncontrollably, I had already left.

Since I didn't even have an explanation for myself, much alone the females I had met a few hours earlier, I hadn't provided one and didn't want to.

It would be an understatement to say that I was ashamed. When my feelings ultimately overcame my senses and I finally took the jump, I was so certain that I was straight and that I was only experiencing these things out of curiosity and excitement that I was left feeling disturbed and a bit afraid.

I had always lived my life in just this manner, which may have been the reason Steve had left me.

I've always been afraid to do new things, and when I finally worked up the guts to do so, I would immediately take several steps back and never try the item again. At the time, this was precisely how I was feeling.

Even after learning all this, I still wanted to bolt from the cabin and never see the girls again because I did not want to upset the balance or add to my already difficult life. I had enjoyed the kiss, in fact, I had enjoyed it so much that had Mia not climaxed then, I would have tried slipping in a tongue or tried cupping a feel of Mia's beautiful breasts.

My train of thinking was broken by a knock at the door.

I murmured, attempting to collect myself, "Come in."

Mia answered.

I would have chosen Lucy over the girl I had just passionately kissed before fleeing into a room like a terrified little chicken.

Mia, who was just wearing a jacket and boots after Lucy had savagely torn her summer dress off of her, begged Lucy if she may sit next to her.

I answered, "Yes, but before you say anything, I want to say something," as

Mia sat next to me and I breathed in the lovely scent of her body. "You and Lucy are totally different from me. In fact, I doubt that we would have ever met if my fiancée hadn't ever broken up with me. A catastrophe in my life was necessary to motivate me to visit a club. That's how unique I am. I have to be intimidated into leaving my home, and I detest change, so everything that transpired tonight has left me feeling very bewildered and quite afraid. I have lost track of who I am. I had hoped that tonight would mark the beginning of a new chapter in my life—one in which I would know exactly what I wanted and how to obtain it. Instead, I find myself sitting in a cabin in the middle of nowhere, more perplexed than ever and with more questions than answers.

"How did the kiss feel?" Mia spoke with a warm, sweet voice.

"I did."

"So, in that case, you shouldn't have any questions. You gave a girl a kiss and enjoyed it. There is a whole song about it by Kate Perry.

However, I find it difficult to warm up to change due to my nature. Back home, I had a child. What does any of this even mean? Do I now need to start looking for dates with women? Will my child be raised by two mothers?"

Don't get ahead of yourself, Amaya, oh my goodness. You loved kissing a female. That does not imply that you are a lesbian or that your child would experience bullying at school as a result of having two moms. I believe you ought to further explore this aspect of yourself. Do you know what the best thing about adventure is? Think of it as a thrilling voyage. Mia questioned while holding my hand in one hand and the upper one in the other.

That one ring generally falls into Mount Doom at the conclusion?

Mia chuckled. Yes, but only if you are a hobbit, and based on the way you appear, you are not a hobbit. You have the appearance of an elf—a lovely, magical elf. The wonderful thing about adventures, as I said, is that they never make you feel as if you squandered your time. What could be more wonderful than that? All experiences enhance your personality, and this one may even add a whole gender to the individuals you can have sex with.

As Mia stated this and looked into my eyes, I was unexpectedly astounded by her maturity and intelligence. This beauty had just shown how deeply she could think, while I was expected to be the one with the child and behave like a parent.

I have to go right now. My boyfriend's pickup vehicle is outside waiting for me.

Have a boyfriend, please? I questioned, unable to contain my amazement in my tone.

"Yes. You don't have to choose one gender, as I previously said. You may only choose the individual.

But I thought you loved Lucy, right?

Nevertheless, is she?

I didn't have a response for it or one that Mia would like.

"Exactly. You can't always get what you want in life, so you have to settle with Harvard grads who drive pickup trucks while you wait.

"That is an odd pairing. I smiled and added, "I don't think of pick-up trucks when I think of Harvard grads.

"Well, he's strange. Anyway, I'm going to leave the cabin for you and Lucy, and if you were to heed my advise, I'd say you should use this evening to go on the trip we discussed.

However, won't you mind?

"No. I am aware that she sleeps with stupid bitches. She will now at least sleep with someone I like. And who knows, I could even join you on that expedition someday," Mia smirked before standing up, "a farewell kiss?"

This time, I acted without thinking. The moment my lips touched Mia's and I felt the delightful sensation of butterflies flying in my stomach, I understood I was ready to go on an adventure. I too stood up, bent forward, and kissed Mia.

Lucy questioned as Mia exited the cabin and headed up to the pickup vehicle with the headlights on, "What were you guys talking about?"

The question is, "What do you think?" We saw the vehicle perform a U-turn and drive out into the woods while I responded.

I believe she was attempting to persuade you to let me fuck you, Lucy said as she turned around and entered the cabin. I followed.

"Aren't you always so direct with your words?"

Lucy remarked, "I don't believe in wasting time, but I'm right, aren't I?"

"No. She wasn't attempting to persuade me to take any action. All she spoke about was logic.

"Yup, that's what she is good at, talking logic, but when it comes to her, all logic is thrown out the window."

I walked over to the sofa and slumped down, saying, "She truly loves you, you know.

And I adore her too, just as I love all other lovely, young, 18-year-old blondes who resemble Loren Gray," Lucy said as she reached for a huge bottle of whiskey from one of the built-in cupboards over the kitchenette.

Lucy carried the bottle over to the sofa and poured two cocktails for us. "Now that the young one has left, let us get down to the real drinks," she said.

I took the drink from her hand and apologized for the difficult upbringing you had.

No, I'm not. I am proud of that person because it helped me become who I am now. I can ride superbikes, kick anybody in the ass, and have any women I want in my bed. What more could I ask for?

"Love, maybe?" I spoke those words in the hopes of hearing an immediate reply, but Lucy only smiled sadly and replied, "I really think I need that. Who doesn't, after all?

"So why don't you go after it?" I questioned while leaning in close and examining Lucy's face intently, attempting to discern any cues she may be giving out that her speech might not, but possibly her face just might.

"Tell me, if you pursue it, is it really love?"

I'd never heard anything so accurate. The more I considered what Lucy had just said, the more sense it seemed to make.

Love was supposed to be discovered, but not by searching. Love that was not sought was love more pure than any other, and people were destined to stumble upon it.

"However, you don't allow yourself the chance to look for it. You deliberately avoid situations where you could accidentally fall in love.

Please elucidate, Lucy said as she furrowed her brow and glared at me with a perplexed face. How can I intentionally prevent myself from finding myself in circumstances where falling in love is impossible?

I said, immediately regretting the final part of my sentence, "By looking for random one-night stands, by fucking a girl, but not making love to her, by forcing them to ride superbikes and nearly killing them before you can begin to fall for them."

So if I hadn't had you ride that bike, there was a possibility that you may fall in love with me? You ought to have informed me that earlier. With wide eyes and an exuberant tone, Lucy continued, "We could have taken an Uber or anything.

I tucked a strand of hair behind my ear and looked outside at the swaying trees while feeling Lucy's gaze burn a hole in the side of my face. "I did not say there was a chance, all I said was, if I were a girl more inclined towards the female gender, you would have killed me before even getting to know me," I said.

"I recognize your current tendency...I saw your kissing of Mia. I would hazard a guess that you are more than merely inclined," Lucy scooted closer, and I kept my gaze focused on the outdoors while doing my best to avoid Lucy's mesmerizing blue eyes.

I told Lucy what I had told Mia, adding, "I don't know any more."

Lucy put a hand on my arm and softly stroked the side, saying, "Well, let me help you with that."

My neck developed goosebumps, and a chill ran up my spine.

A tuft of cloud covered the moon, and for a brief moment, the woods outside were obscured by pitch-blackness as the moonlight vanished and enveloped the area around the cabin.

"Not yet," I murmured, pushing Lucy's hand away. "I don't want to explore with someone who only wants to fuck me hard," I said. I want to experience this for the first time with a kind person who will respect that it is my first time and won't overwhelm me.

When I watched Lucy's eye light up in anger, the fire rapidly subsided and was replaced by a fog of grief. After taking her hand from my arm and saying, "I can do that as well," she rose up and went up to the window. She turned her back on me and said, "I want to show you something," as I stared out the window and felt my eyes caress the contours of her hips and take in the look of her toned figure.

I remarked, attempting to lighten the situation, "I have already seen more than I anticipated I would see tonight.

Lucy swung around and stared at me, "No, nothing sexual, nothing that would overwhelm you," "Let's take a short stroll."

***

Lucy still hadn't informed me where we were headed after fifteen minutes of us strolling through the woods.

"Listen, please tell me whether you are a serial murderer who targets heterosexual females who refuse to have sex with you. I replied, moving a low-hanging branch out of my face, "I am willing to have sex with you to save my life.

"Amaya, I believe you need to be more afraid of woodchucks than of my murdering you. Lucy squeezed my leg and said, "I still can't get over how you almost wet your pants when an animal no larger than your hand crossed your path.

Hey, I don't smack people about at clubs. And I had no idea whether it was a wolf or a woodchuck. In my opinion, it may have been an extraterrestrial sent to conquer the earth.

"Well, now that you've brought it up, allow me to introduce myself. So, I'm from Mars originally, Lucy said before laughing out loud.

I said, scanning the woodland for any indication of woodchucks, "It's good that you enjoy your own jokes."

"I keep myself entertained," Lucy replied.

After a short while of more walking, it abruptly came into view.

The watchtower was nearly four times taller than the tallest tree in the area, rising out from the tangle of trees like a wooden skyscraper towering over a field of green. Behind the watchtower, the moon shined like a lantern suspended in the sky.

"Don't you dare tell me we're going to climb that?" My finger was on the tower.

Lucy tapped her bag, which I now knew housed her camera, and added, "Yes, my dear, we are going to climb that, and then, we are going to have a little photo shoot."

The ascent wasn't as terrifying as I had anticipated. There was a wooden railing that you could grab onto as you ascended the large steps leading to the turret.

I questioned, "Who built this?"

God is aware. I was in need of a cigarette when I first arrived to Mia's cabin, so I wandered around the woods and found upon this little gem, which I climbed to the top of. Nobody knows where it is, and I doubt Mia even knows.

Why didn't you tell her, I wonder?

"Because I wanted to keep the location secret for myself, and now, when I am tired of this world, when I just need to get away from everything," she said.

We eventually made it to the top, which was a big wooden platform without a guardrail, and when I stopped and turned to look about, the vista really astounded me.

Far off, to my right, I could see a lake, its blue waters reflecting the moonlight, and even further, rising from the forest, was a small hill, a lone figure standing tall amidst the sea of green. The trees were illuminated by the moonlight, their tops gently swaying in the moisture-laden winds.

I could only utter, "This is beautiful," as I stood still in the presence of such majesty.

Lucy was entirely unfazed by the beauty all around her and kept her eyes fixed just on me as I turned to gaze at her.

She said, "Yup, it truly is a thing of beauty," and I flushed as I saw her eyes roving over my body.

I said, "You mentioned something about a picture shoot.

"Yes," Lucy said, shaking her head as if to rouse herself from her reverie. She then started to unzip her luggage.

She took out her DSLR camera and placed it on the ground. She then took out a bedsheet from her bag, yanked it open, and spread it out evenly on the floor.

She touched the bedsheet and called out to me, "Come."

"What? I questioned, "Will I be the focus of this picture shoot?

The question, "Who else?"

I replied, sitting on the bed sheet, "Okay, but I'm not going to take off my clothes."

Lucy responded, playing with the buttons on her camera, "We will see about that.

I had a peek around while Lucy set up the camera. With the majesty of God's creation all around us, it was absolutely amazing up there, and I questioned whether or not it was something that we as humans took for granted to be in the presence of nature.

I, for one, couldn't recall the last time I left the concrete jungle of New York and just let myself get lost in the great outdoors.

I never considered organizing a vacation to the woods because I lacked the desire to do it, not because I didn't have enough time. It was because I had forgotten what it was like to breathe in fresh air and feel just pure, unadulterated wind on my face.

Lucy's words drew me back to the present, where I would soon stand for the camera, something I had never done before. "Okay, we are all set," she said.

I felt like a complete moron, so I responded, "Okay, but I have no idea what to do." For a little moment, I felt envious of Mia and worried that Lucy could think poorly of me since I was reminded of how well trained he was and how completely natural Mia looked in front of the camera.

"Amaya, your beauty will take care of everything. You don't need to do anything, Lucy remarked, pressing a camera button as I heard a "click."

"Just follow my instructions and don't think about the other person who is with you. Imagine being alone yourself.

It was easier said than done, particularly when the companion you were meant to forget about had unexpectedly developed feelings for you.

I heard Lucy's voice, "Amaya, look up at the moon," and I complied.

Several additional clicks were audible.

"Now, look at me."

I turned to face the camera.

The camera, not. Observe me. Look into my eyes, Lucy commanded.

Fuck.

gazing into Lucy's eyes was more difficult than gazing at the camera.

I prayed and hoped that my anxiety didn't show on my face.

"Now softly extend your left leg while maintaining that curled-up position for your right. Let it peek out from your skirt's slit.

I went above and above. I hoisted my skirt till it reached my thighs and my left leg was visible.

"Perfect. Keep your eyes on me," Lucy said as I became more assured with each passing second.

Posing for the camera gave me a sense of freedom. I immediately felt like flaunting my body and recognizing and enjoying the beauty I had been given was the correct thing to do.

I knelt down and carefully removed the strap off my top. I then bent my head to the left and opened my lips sensually.

Within a few feet of me, I saw Lucy's eyes dilate as her fingers hurriedly worked on the camera.

Then, in order to prevent my top from dropping, I slipped the second strap off of my other shoulder as well.

I merely needed to release my hand for it to drop, showing Lucy and the camera my boobs.

I overheard Lucy saying, "Fuck," to herself.

I said with a sneaky grin, "Do you want me to let go?"

Lucy pleaded, "Oh fuck yes, baby," and I appreciated the nickname she gave me more than the desperate tone of her voice.

I wonder, "What do I get in return?"

"Whatever you want," was the prompt response.

I said, "Take off your top as well."

As her lovely breasts were revealed, Lucy quickly unhooked her bralette and let it fall to the ground.

I was awestruck by how beautiful and flawless they were.

They weren't enormous, nor were they diminutive. They were just ideal.

Her nipples, standing upright and drenched in moonlight, were demanding to be licked. Her areolas were a shade of rose pink.

I licked my lips as Lucy gave one of her nipples a little squeeze while holding it between her finger and thumb.

I grumbled.

"Your turn," she commanded.

I inhaled deeply while keeping my gaze fixed on Lucy's breast. After that, I released go of my top and my hand slid to the ground.

My nipples also sprang up straight when I first felt the breeze on them.

The second thing I noticed was Lucy's facial reaction.

I took great pleasure in the impact I was making on Lucy, who was stooping with the camera loosely in one hand, her mouth wide, and her eyes riveted on my tits.

After that, I did exactly what Lucy had done.

I moaned softly while teasing my nipple between my fingers as pleasure flooded my body.

Lucy also screamed quite loud.

"Amaya, you are fucking teasing me. Right now, I fucking hate you," said Lucy.

I groaned more this time and added, "The photo shoot was your idea," while squeezing my breast with my palm.

"I'd want to give you a hug. Let me at least feel them on my own chest and on my flesh. Please, just a hug. If I refused Lucy's request, I was afraid she would start weeping.

The temptation to say yes was strong since Lucy was acting precisely way I had wanted her to—without the pressure or desire to be in charge.

On her knees, this fiery-tempered girl—a classic dominatrix—begged for nothing more than a hug.

I paused before responding, "Okay, but just a hug," and I questioned why I had been so reluctant to let things continue.

I had already gone beyond every restriction I had placed on myself, and if I had allowed a hug and exposed my breasts, I could have easily gone much farther, but something still prevented me from letting go and letting myself be free.

Lucy, however, did not wait for me to reconsider. She came at me while crawling on her knees, throwing her arms around me, pressing her bare chest against mine, and tightly hugging me.

I was immediately turned on as she rubbed the side of her face against mine and let out a long, contented moan.

I gave the girl a bear hug in return, encircling her in my arms as I groaned.

The first time I felt another girl's tits against mine, our boobs pressed against one other, and the sensation was beyond gorgeous.

It was so wonderful for me that I could not help but whisper Lucy's name in her ear. I could feel our nipples rubbing against one another and I could feel her heart racing against my skin.

"Amaya…" Lucy groaned in response, and she then began desperately grabbing my back.

I could only throw my head back, shut my eyes, and let the waves of ecstasy wash over my body until she abruptly placed her lips on the side of my neck and kissed me lovingly, pushing my skin between them.

Every time Lucy cried out my name, she planted a kiss on my neck. Then, after what felt like an eternity, she moved to kiss my chin, followed by kissing my jawline, and finally, she reached my mouth. When our lips collided, our hands clung to each other's bodies as if our lives depended on it.

"Aaaahhhh…." When I felt Lucy's fingertips on my breast, I groaned out.

For as long as she could, Lucy had fought to maintain her composure, but now she had snapped.

Amaya was enjoying every minute of her hands rubbing her breast harder than before.

Lucy was to be as harsh as she could make her.

They eventually heard it.

The gunshot sounded out like a threatening blast of cloud, piercing the silence of the air.

Lucy pulled go of me and quickly looked around, asking, "What the fuck was that?"

As Lucy stood up, my heart was already in my throat, and I felt every nerve in my body numb as I froze.

Bang

As soon as another shot was fired, I instinctively grabbed Lucy's hand.

Lucy said, "Put on your clothes."

Something had piqued her interest.

As Lucy continued to wear her bralette, I hastened to put on my top.

I could see Lucy gazing at something from where I was standing on the platform, but I had no idea what.

I became more aware of what had Lucy's attention as I got closer to the brink.

Two headlights illuminated a stand of trees in the night somewhere in the midst of the woodland.

The question was, "What do you think it was?" Standing close to Lucy, I questioned.

"That was a gunshot, and I think it came from there," Lucy remarked, pointing at the headlights.

In an instant, Lucy grabbed my wrist and said loudly, "I think I know what vehicle that is," before abruptly turning around, sprinting across the platform, and beginning to descend the steps. She said, "Follow me, but keep your distance," and I reacted immediately.

*** Lucy could run faster than me, so I had to use all of my effort to keep her in view as she scurried between tree trunks and branches, closing up on the truck that we had been able to see from the top of the watchtower.

I didn't understand why we were heading in its direction if Lucy was correct and the gunshot had come from someplace close to the car.

However, I did not want to be abandoned in the middle of the forest, so my only choice was to follow Lucy and cross my fingers.

My heart was pounding in my chest as I sprinted into the trees when I realized I could no longer see Lucy.

"Lucy!" I yelled, but nobody responded.

"LUCY!" I yelled even louder, but deathly quiet followed.

The only sounds I could hear were the sound of my own breathing and the infrequent rustle of the leaves as the wind blew through the trees.

Cold perspiration started to form in beads on my forehead as I worried.

I began to feverishly scan the area, dashing back and forth while yelling "Lucy!" as tears streamed down my eyes.

My skirt tore at the bottom after getting entangled in a prickly shrub, and the sound sent chills through my body.

After circling for a while, I finally realized I was lost and needed to calm down if I wanted to locate Lucy again.

I remained still while listening for any sound that would lead me in the correct way, but all I could hear was the eerie quiet of the forest.

Then I heard the sound of approaching footsteps and the rustle of leaves.

I exhaled deeply and decided that this was it.

In a matter of minutes, I had gone from being utterly delighted to being utterly terrified, and now that I was starting to try to change, I was about to be shot in the midst of the forest.

I stood motionless with my eyes closed, preparing to welcome death.

Lucy's voice, when she spoke, "Amaya," had never sounded more endearing.

As soon as I opened my eyes, I saw Lucy standing a few steps away from me, Mia's hand slung over her shoulder, and her legs badly wounded.

"Oh, my God!" I screamed. "Oh my god, oh my god, oh my god," I wished I had passed away. I saw Lucy's lips was bleeding as she carried Mia approach me, and the worry of it all was worse than death.

As Mia cried out in anguish, Lucy remarked, "Amaya, I urge you to calm down. The only thing you need to do is be silent, Lucy said.

But what just happened? I whispered.

"Our girl here had a little bit of a fight with her boyfriend, and it turns out, he has anger issues."

"So, he shot her?" you ask. I said in horror.

"Yes, however, missed. Then he attempted to shoot her again as our braveheart here was trying to pull the pistol from his grasp. We heard a second gunshot after that. Fortunately, I was able to strike him in the jaw just in time.

Despite hearing what Lucy was saying, I couldn't seem to process what she was saying. I just nodded, waiting for Lucy to give me instructions.

Come, assist me in bringing her fatass back to the cabin.

***

We were quickly lifting Mia onto the bed in the bedroom thanks to the fact that the cabin was just a 10-minute walk from where I had discovered Lucy and Mia.

What happened to the boyfriend? I instantly had the thought to inquire.

Lucy remarked, "I tied him to his seat with the seatbelt," as if she did it every Sunday.

I said, "Okay," since I had no better words to say at the time.

"Mia... I've already made a 911 call. They will arrive soon, but before they do, you must be sincere with them. You cannot continue to mislead everyone about him. That guy is a risk to you and to society since he has serious anger management difficulties. You're not allowed to see him any more.

Mia gave a head nod.

I responded, "We have to stop the bleeding.

Lucy said, "On it," and tore a piece of fabric from the bedsheet's corner, tying it around the bullet hole.

I questioned, "Where is the bullet?"

"I took it out,"

"Lucy, who the heck are you? A covert agent? I questioned, "How do you know how to remove a bullet from someone's body?" in utter incredulity.

She tied the knot, blocking the blood flow, and said, "Because I removed one from my own a long time ago, that should do the work.

I questioned, "What if he frees himself and comes after us?"

Amaya, he won't. The cops are already on the way, and he won't be waking up from his nap any time soon. Please take a little break now while we wait outside, okay?

Mia muttered, "Okay.

As I kissed her forehead and murmured, "Take care, Mia," she sat up.

I'm sorry for interfering with your experience, Mia said with a grin as she rubbed her lips together.

How are you doing?

Lucy informed me.

Don't worry about it, I see. You try to relax right now, okay?

***

After pouring herself a drink of whiskey, Lucy exclaimed, "Well, that was close," and quickly finished the whole glass.

I responded, hands crossed over my breast, "You are wounded too, Lucy.

"This is meaningless. Don't stress about it.

"Lucy, you are a great lady. I mean, I doubt I'll ever run across someone quite like you again.

Lucy grinned and drained the glass once again. "Never say never," she said.

"No, I'm not kidding. In your eyes, I am nothing. I spoke more softly to myself than to Lucy when I said, "I am weak, easily startled, and good for nothing.

"You are fine, Amaya," Lucy remarked.

"No, I couldn't even have the courage to just break away tonight. I was always being held back by these notions.

After approaching me and giving me a direct look, Lucy said, "Now that you know this, what are you going to do about it?"

I commanded them to stop being afraid, but just then, distant police sirens shattered the silence.

***

Will she be alright? I enquired as Lucy closed the door and headed back to the sofa, where I was seated holding a beverage.

"Yes," Lucy said as she slouched down on the sofa next to me.

"I still believe we ought to have accompanied her."

Lucy responded, "She didn't want us to.

"Why?"

She mentioned an excursion somewhere. I was unable to understand it in any way.

I grinned.

What happens next? Lucy was sitting on the sofa with her legs crossed, staring at me with interest while her face was in her hands.

I said, "Fuck me, Lucy," Like you do with other females, fuck me. I added, taking off my top for the second time that night, "In fact, I want you to give me your best.

What if you wanted me to treat you gently since this was your first time? Lucy remarked, staring longingly at me.

"Screw that. I dropped my top in the trash and sat with my hands in my lap, waiting for Lucy to move. "I might have just had a near-death experience, and I would be a fool if I were to still take things slowly," I said.

Are you certain? As she drew nearer, Lucy put her hand on the side of my face.

I exhaled, "Yes," and felt my heartbeat pick up.

There it was.

I could not be happier that I had given myself to the beast.

Don't say I didn't ask you, Lucy said before abruptly slipping her hand away from my face and slipping it into my hair.

With a start, Lucy sprang onto my lap and crossed her legs around my waist before grabbing my hair in a hand.

Lucy wrenched my head back, "You can always tap out," and I felt the first sting of agony.

Accepted, but I won't.

Lucy reached out and licked my side of the face. I have never seen a lady with a more beautiful face than you have, Fuck me, Amaya," Lucy moaned, and I could feel her passion growing. Lucy added, "I could just eat you whole," and then she seized my face in both of her hands and licked my lips.

I was the object of play. Right now, all Lucy saw in me was an object—an object of want, an item she intended to exploit to get the most pleasure possible—and the notion of being used as such made my pussy leak.

"Eat me whole," I want you to say. I belong to you; I am yours. As Lucy got hold of my tits and squeezed them, I groaned.

But I believed you to be straight," My breasts were feeling more pressure from

Lucy, and it was the most delightful feeling in the world.

I had always believed that my body was delicate, so I expected to feel agony as Lucy pushed on my breasts, but all I felt was lingering pressure and a tingling in my pussy that was intensifying with every passing second.

I was then drawn in for a kiss after that.

Rather than a kiss, it seemed more like an attack on my mouth.

Mouths shot wide, tongues snaked out, and they clashed in a lust-filled struggle as Lucy fervently began to lick the interior of my mouth.

My body was hit by a series of frantic bliss waves as I felt my senses being overwhelmed by demands.

Desires are worse and more filthy than I could have ever dreamed or considered.

I had desires that I believed were beyond my understanding, and one of them was to tear open Lucy's bralette the same way she had torn open Mia's summer dress.

I grabbed hold of her bralette's straps with both of my hands as her mouth was sucking on my lips and tongue and tugged it away from her body without releasing the hooks in the back.

For a brief while, Lucy had to pause from kissing me to groan. After that, she pulled my hair harder than before, and this time, I could feel the agony.

You want to participate in the game, too? I was forced to gaze into Lucy's eyes as she hushed, "You want to get naughty as well as well all of a sudden?" The way Lucy was gritting her teeth and staring intently into my eyes made me feel threatened.

"Yesss…" I sighed and totally gave my body over to Lucy, not bothering to disguise the hints of hopelessness and desperation that were seething under my tone.

Lucy told me to "open your mouth," and I did as she asked.

Lucy continued, "Stick your pretty tongue out."

I carried out the request.

Lucy said, "Good girl," and spat a drop of saliva onto my tongue before violently clamping my jaws together and forcing me to swallow the substance.

I took a swallow before opening my lips again and said, "More. I want more. I want to drink more," Lucy said as she gripped my neck and spit in my face.

"Moreeee…"

I had no idea what had me in its grip.

It was as if a ghost, who hadn't had sex in millions of years, had taken possession of me and had all the sex it desired in a single night.

What the heck has happened to you all of a sudden, Lucy said with a raised eyebrow and her signature sneer on her face?

I required Lucy's saliva to moisten my dry throat as I said, "I don't know," in a scratchy voice.

Lucy grabbed me by the hair, pulled me across the sofa, and told me to lay on my stomach. "Come here, you fucking slut," she said.

She then seized my skirt's waistline with her two fingers and pulled it down completely in one motion.

My ass was exposed, and Lucy was massaging and squeezing it while gazing at it urgently. It was the most sexual sight I had ever seen.

All night long, this ass has been tempting me. Ever since I met you, Amaya, I have been having nasty fucking ideas about it.

It is now in your line of sight. I looked over my shoulder and enjoyed the desire in Lucy's eyes as I continued, "bared and exposed as it has never been in front of anybody else but my fiancée.

"Fuck that scumbag. When Lucy remarked, "How the fuck did he ever leave this," she grabbed my ass and gave it a hard bounce.

The subsequent scene I saw, though, stayed in my mind for a very long time.

As she began licking my ass cleavage like a wicked old guy having sex with a young, sexy girl and making guttural, urgent noises with her throat, Lucy gave me the impression that she was a crazy addicted to sex.

I moaned and began stroking my pussy on the couch's fabric.

The vision I saw was too sexual and hot, and my pussy was too irritated to be touched.

I began stroking my clit as Lucy pulled my legs forward and forced me into a dog-like pose. As I worked as hard as I could to touch my pussy, Lucy began kissing my thighs and legs until she pushed my hand away and replaced it with her tongue.

Her tongue made its first contact with my pussy, sending vibrations through my whole body. I had to hold the couch's armrests and bite down on my wrist to resist screaming like a woman being tortured to death.

I had to scream as Lucy began to lick my pussy with protracted, forceful strokes of her tongue.

The sound of my groans and Lucy's quiet whimpers echoed throughout the cottage.

My pussy was covered in saliva from her tongue, which combined with the fluids from my own pussy to produce an extremely sexual concoction that Lucy began to gulp.

I sighed, "Aaaahhhhh this is...so...fucking....gooooodd."

I could feel my orgasm coming on with each prod of Lucy's tongue.

I gasped at the suddenness of Lucy's move as she quickly continued by sticking a finger up my vagina.

Lucy knew exactly what she was doing as she pumped her finger in and out of my clit, flicked it, and even bit on it with just the tip of her teeth.

Do you want to make me into a dyke like you, you fucking....bitch? Huh? I backed up and exclaimed, "Why the fuck does this feel so fucking......aaahhhh...amazing,"
attempting to take in as much of Lucy's finger up my cunt as I possibly could.

"Yes. You should work as my personal lesbian slave, I want you to. And after that, I want to use a strap-on to fuck your pussy raw on camera. We will then email that footage to your worthless ex-fiance. Let him discover what he was missing. Luch continued, murmuring into my pussy lips and speeding up her thrusts, "Let him see what a freak his future wife may have been.

The room was filled with the squelching sound of my extremely wet vagina as it welcomed the blonde's lovely fingers.

But suddenly, as if hit by a lightning in the center of the ground, I felt my body shake, my thoughts go numb, and I saw darkness obstruct my vision.

The demon with blonde hair and a face like Natalie Dormer chuckled, pleased with her job as I spasmed, thrashing my legs in the air, and attempting to grasp onto anything I could find. With my loudest scream yet, I screamed louder than I had ever before.

***

My breathing was rapid, and my forehead was wet.

A stunning young blonde was holding me from behind as she was also nude, her breasts stroking against my back. Suddenly, Lucy and I were lying together while the leaves outside rustled.

"They say all a girl needs to turn into a lesbian is a feminine tongue in her pussy, a shaking orgasm, and then a cuddle with bodies stuck together, hair tangled together, and heartbeats synced with each other."

"I don't believe our hearts are beating in time right now. Yours must be much slower than mine. I laughed and turned over to face Lucy before wrapping my legs around her little waist, saying, "I'm sorry, I don't think you have converted me after all, but I will say this, I think I might be addicted."

"What for?"

Now that I had came and the crazy had left me, I was hesitant to use the term pussy. "To having a feminine tongue in my pussy," I said.

Having her fingers play with my nipples, Lucy questioned, "Every tongue, or just mine?"

Now, it's yours, I said.

"For now?" Lucy questioned.

I hesitantly said, "Yeah, I mean, to be honest, I would want to feel Mia's tongue on my pussy as well.

"Oh, you mischievous girl. You'll have to make do with mine for the time being, but I believe I can make that happen," remarked Lucy before giving me a bear embrace.

Ultimately, Lucy had been correct; she had saved my night.

Chapter Three

It had been two hours since Peyton had dropped Stella at the beach, and although the girls had expected there to be a crowd at the beach, there were hardly any people as it was a working day. Stella actually liked that.

She wanted to enjoy the sound of the waves, and the serenity of the ocean without crying kids, and teenage girls doing their TikTok dances.

But two hours is a long time, and Stella had started to get a little bored as time went on.

She took a long walk beside the crashing waves, built herself a little sandcastle, and made two miniature sand figures of her and Peyton, holding hands, and then realized how cringy that was, and proceeded to destroy them before Peyton showed up.

And as time stretched, her anxiety grew as well.

She was alone on the beach, and although Peyton had made sure they were not followed by anyone, Stella could not help but fear an attack out of nowhere, and she kept turning her head back, and kept looking over her shoulder to see if there was a shady character lurking behind the palm trees, waiting for an opportunity to pounce on her.

After about half an hour more of nervously prowling the beach, Stella found a family of four, and made sure she was close enough to them the entire time.

Stella was feeling drowsy as she sat behind a palm tree, but just as she was ready to nod off, she caught sight of a guy in the heat of the sun wearing a hooded sweatshirt with the hood up.

Stella's heart awoke and began to race.

Stella got to her feet and saw there was no one around for miles after the family departed the beach.

Stella could feel her panic growing as the guy moved closer to her, approaching at a rate only a bit faster than a brisk stroll.

Stella heard Peyton's voice behind her say, "Don't worry, he's a cop."

As soon as Stella turned back and saw Peyton's happy face, she felt a rush of comfort sweep over her. As Peyton laughed, Stella hugged Peyton tightly in her relief and delight.

Why are you laughing so loudly? Stella continued to cling on Peyton while saying, "I was terrified to death.

Peyton said, putting her hand over her face to shield it from the light, "Because you embraced me and I laugh anytime I am pleased.

Peyton took Stella's hand and drew her away from the shore, urging them both to go.

***

Stella enquired, "Will you tell me now?"

"Yes, of course I will."

"Well?"

Yes, Mark's arrest has a warrant out for his arrest.

"Seriously? You must be kidding, right?

"I'm not," you say.

"The man exposed him?"

It wasn't him. He claimed to be a mechanic and to operate out of a garage a few kilometers from your home. He said that when he got to the restaurant, he saw you and that you drew his attention. He denied having any connection to Mark and even that he had ever met him. And when we examined his file, we were unable to discover any proof linking the two."

"Then?"

"Well, I knew for sure that Mark had hired this man because my guy had followed him, but since it was an unofficial trail, I can't use it as evidence. So, I hacked his social media accounts, and while we initially were unable to find anything there, we were able to find a few photos on Instagram that the man had archived rather than deleted, and in those photos, the man was standing next to Mark, grinning widely. I knew we had him as soon as I saw that photo.

"God, oh God. To rape me, Mark had hired a man, right?

Yes, and the guy broke down and told us everything when we showed him the evidence and informed him that his charges will be changed from burglary to attempted rape. He said that Mark despises you so much that he would hire a hitman to assassinate you.

Stella's shock at what she had just heard was palpable.

Have I murdered you? Why? Simply because I didn't share a bed with him?

"No, it seems that this is complex. The guy said that Mark dislikes you for some other reason. The cause of which not even he is aware.

"What?"

"I was hoping you could clarify that for me?" For the first time, Stella saw a strange expression in Peyton's eye as she gave her an inquiring stare that wasn't frightening but also wasn't nice.

"Peyton, I don't understand a word the guy is saying. Only a week had passed since I began working with Mark, and that was when he first arrived to the restaurant and set eyes on me. The next day, he attempted to get a bit more physical, and when I declined, he smacked me across the face, which is when I decided to stop. Nothing else took place.

Just a few more seconds passed while Peyton continued to look at Stella before the young policeman responded, "I know nothing more occurred. I just wanted to hear your thoughts on the subject. So Stella, South Carolina Shakira, how do you feel about how I did? And how does it feel to finally feel that justice has been served?

"I still find it hard to believe that Mark's arrest is being sought; I never thought,"

three loud bangs.

Peyton's car's tires were fired at with three gunshots that tore through the air.

Before Peyton intervened, the automobile had drifted off the road and was heading straight for a tree.

The vehicle abruptly stopped in the midst of a patch of dry bushes that extended as far as the eye could see on either side of the road.

Peyton's automobile was stuck in a no-man's-land with another vehicle obstructing the way.

BANG, BANG.

Two additional shots were fired, one of which just missed Peyton's face and struck the back seat before striking the windshield.

Say "Get Down!" Stella was forced to squat on the floor of the vehicle after Peyton yelled at her and pushed her head down.

Using the door as cover, Peyton slipped out after unlocking the door on her side.

After a little period of stillness, she glanced over the door and saw two males, one behind the car's trunk with just his eyes visible over the bonnet and the other in a similar position behind the bonnet.

Peyton counted the number of rounds in her pistol.

3. "Fuck!" After her shooting practice, Peyton shouted, hating the need to reload her ammunition.

Peyton was fired at by the guy hiding behind the bonnet, but the bullet missed Peyton and instead struck the side of the door.

Stella, who was still squatting down with her eyes wide in terror and her face etched with despair, caught Peyton's attention.

Peyton was aware that she needed to eliminate them both simultaneously. She just had three bullets to do it.

Peyton waited for the shooter to reload.

BANG!

Peyton raised her head above the door, took aim, and fired her own pistol after the guy had fired.

Due to the hissing sound the bullet created as it exited the muzzle, her rifle made less noise.

The gunshot entered his forehead before the guy behind the bonnet realized what was happening.

Another attempt.

The only sounds that broke the stillness were Stella's heavy breathing and the whistling of the bushes in the wind. Peyton also killed the second guy, and everything was done in a matter of minutes.

***

Stella repeated, "I am fine," for the eleventh time in the last thirty minutes as Peyton drove the vehicle to Stella's house.

"You did fantastic, Stella," Peyton replied. "You continued to be quite powerful even after the cops came. You performed a lot better than previously," Peyton replied, looking straight ahead.

"I'm tired of feeling terrified. I've had it with being the weakling.

"You were never weak," Peyton added.

However, I was. Trust me, I was.

"What has changed now?"

"Something is different. I sense it. I felt pathetically weak as bullets flew all about me as my unconsciousness started to choke me once again. Then, you were in front of me. You are younger than me, brave, and exhibit no sign of fear. You are also much more resilient. Stella turned to Peyton and said, "You've inspired me, Peyton.

Peyton muttered, "I was doing my job.

And you did a fantastic job.

So let's hope. We now have enough evidence against Mark to put him behind bars for a while. I simply don't understand why he would take such drastic measures to harm you.

Stella said, "I have no notion.

"I'm glad you're all right."

Why would I not be? Stella said, "I had you with me," and continued to hold Peyton's hand as she peered out the window.

***

Stella put her flat door key in the keyhole and unlocked it.

There were a lot of lilies in the house, and Peyton enjoyed going into Stella's home and smelling something that had grown to be so familiar to Stella.

"I should also plant some lilies in my home. Your home usually smells amazing, and I truly like that.

Stella pulled Peyton up against the wall, interrupting her.

What about you smells even better? Stella rubbed her nose in Peyton's hair and whispered, "Your hair..." She then loosened Peyton's ponytail and allowed her hair flow freely.

Your body... Stella proceeded, smelling Peyton's neck before licking her collarbone and making her first lip contact with her flesh.

"Stella?" Without thinking, Peyton put her hand into Stella's hair as she closed her eyes and said.

"Are you certain about this?

"I have never been more sure," Stella said, kissing Peyton's neck's side and pressing her body against her to feel every inch of her magnificent form. Stella also tasted Peyton's flesh by licking her neck's side all the way down to her ear lobes.

Stella had never experienced such intense lust.

She was just interested in devouring Peyton.

was to subject her to the most vile treatment possible.

The more Stella felt Peyton's towering body against her own, the more she wanted to pull off her clothing and feel it against her flesh bare. Stella's pussy was already pouring.

Peyton grabbed Stella by the waist, spun her around, pinned her against the wall instead of her, and tore the summer dress off her body. "If you are sure, then let me show you how it is done, baby," she said.

Stella appeared before her rescuer completely undressed in a moment, and Peyton gently started taking her clothes off as well, beginning with the button on her police shirt and working her way down to unzipping her slacks.

Peyton was soon just wearing her underwear, and Stella could feel her feelings for her becoming stronger by the second.

Why can't any other female turn me on as she does?

Why does this lady make me want to lose my mind?

Stella's thoughts was racing, but it was quickly overtaken by Peyton's lips slamming into hers as the two girls opened their mouths and started dancing with their tongues.

Stella began unbuckling her bra as soon as she felt Peyton's tongue in her lips. She then threw her arms around Peyton.

Stella yanked Peyton's bra away from her body and dropped it on the ground because she suddenly had the want to touch Peyton's soft breast against her own skin.

Stella kissed Peyton's face while holding it in her hands, saying, "Fuck, I never realized I could feel this passionately for a girl.

With other females, all I ever wanted to do was fuck them, devour them, and then send them away. "I never knew I could feel anything for anyone," Peyton remarked. However, I want to make love to you, sweetheart. I want to hold you in my arms, kiss you, and lick and taste you.

Stella was already eager from Peyton's remarks, so when she expressed her desires to Stella, Stella knelt down, put Peyton's breast in her mouth, and began frantically sucking it.

"Aaaahhhh...." Peyton groaned as she saw Stella lose her composure and start biting and chewing on her nipples like she had been sucking on ladies' nipples her whole life.

Oh yessss, yes, darling, suck on my tits.

Peyton had never been this excited by just having her tits sucked, but seeing Stella, the gorgeous, curvy, tense lady, open her mouth wide and attempt to cram as much of her tit as possible into her mouth was a sight she had never anticipated.

Peyton put her hand on Stella's back and pulled her face closer to her breast while encouraging her and told her she wanted her tits sucked more forcefully.

While Peyton's boobs were pressing on Stella's nose, she could feel herself suffocating but she was determined not to stop.

She tried her best to win this girl over.

She wanted to express her gratitude to the girl for what she had done.

Without taking her gaze away from Peyton's cleavage, Stella reached up to Peyton's thigh, hooked her finger under the waistband of her pants, and tugged them down.

Stella caressed Peyton's lovely little ass and gave it a squeeze as she closed her eyes and arched her back in ecstasy. Then she gave it another squeeze, and another, and another, until she was grabbing Peyton's ass like a sex-crazed crazy and stuffing her mouth with her breast.

Stella, you look so gorgeous right now. Stella's blonde, wavy hair was brushed out of her eyes by Peyton as she grabbed her chin and murmured, "You look so lovely sucking on my tits.

Peyton responded, "Kiss me," and drew her face away from her tits.

They made kissed once more, and Peyton said in Stella's ear, "Let's go to your bedroom."

***

Peyton went on top of Stella after she had been shoved into the bed.

Peyton murmured with her lips twisting into a sly grin, "I enjoy the view from here.

Stella remarked, reaching out and touching Peyton's sculpted body, feeling her abs pop, and then massaging her breasts with both of her hands. "But I have a better one," she said.

I may have to use my strap-on on you if you keep making me feel uncomfortable like this.

"May need to? I assumed you would apply it. Girl, I haven't had a good fuck in years. And I would adore being fucked by you, my beautiful knight.

Peyton chuckled before kissing Stella's bottom lip and softly biting it with her teeth after being overtaken by a strong urge to taste her lips once again.

She did this while standing with her knees crossed.

Stella pinched Peyton's nipples to her heart's content while pressing and groping Peyton's breasts as if they were about to escape her body if she didn't grasp onto them.

Stella moaned in delight every time Peyton used her tongue to lick and taste her skin, saying, "Now, I start exploring your delicious body," as she kissed Stella along the neck.

Peyton took Stella's tits in her hand for the first time and gave them a very little squeeze at first, her eyes sparkling with delight at the sight of the toy she was about to begin playing with.

These are far larger than yours. Stella's breathing became labored as a result of Peyton's outburst of a question that made her ponder how much of them she could fit in her lips.

moving her tongue up to her navel. Peyton softly kissed Stella's underboob as she got close to her tits. Then, Peyton moved higher and took Stella's nipple in her mouth in one motion, giving it a long, hard suck before letting go and making a "pop" sound. As she did this, Peyton was enjoying the effect her kisses were having on the stunning woman below her. She then kissed all around the curve of the tit, savoring each kiss and enjoying the effect they were having.

Stella writhed and moaned, her horniness intensifying as her pussy gushed.

Stella sulked, her voice hoarse and dry, "You are driving me crazy," she said.

Stella found it incredibly erotic and romantic that a girl who was at least 10 years younger to her, who had twice saved her life, was making her moan and squirm in pleasure, was sucking on her tits like a baby, and calling her "sweetheart." "And so are you," Peyton said.

Please continue sucking my tits, Peyton. Take control of them, baby. Stella had no understanding why she was uttering such passionate words like, "Make me yours.

Did one-night stands participants often use language like this?

Was she acting too sensitively?

How then could she not be?

The gentleman who had saved her life was holding her in his arms.

Oh, other than making you mine, Stella, there is nothing else on my thoughts. I want to get to know you and your lovely physique since you are such a beautiful lady. You won't be leaving me anytime soon.

After saying so, Peyton cupped Stella's nipple with her lips and began bobbing her head up and down while sucking as hard as she could on the blonde's tits, sending shivers of ecstasy through Stella's body.

"OHHHHH FUCKK YESSS PEYTONNNN!"

While her youthful lover went wild on her breasts, Stella shouted, writhed, gripped the sheets in a fist, and arched her body.

Peyton was also in paradise. Her pussy had been pleading with her to make love to Stella ever since she had first set eyes on the stunning lady.

Peyton was feeling raw desire and love, something she had never had with a female before when paired with Stella's goodness and compassion.

Then, the two ladies collapsed into a mass of entangled limbs. Peyton and Stella were slowly beginning to get more passionate toward one another as they were around each other with their hands and sinking their nails into one another's flesh.

Finally, Peyton's need to taste Stella's puss became too strong to deny.

It was prepared for her, she knew.

All she had to do was kiss her way down Stella's body, tormenting and tease Stella with tender kisses till she reached her mound, and then kiss her pussy lips like a lover making love to her paramour. She could already smell Stella's fluids.

And Peyton really carried out that action.

Stella had a loss of consciousness the first time Peyton placed his thick, luscious lips on her pussy, and she briefly believed she was going to faint.

Stella shrieked as her body, which was now beyond of her control, twisted and contorted.

Stella once more moaned as Peyton laughed and rubbed her puss again.

Stella uttered a constant stream of sounds with her lips, "Ah..ah...ah..ah..ah..ah..," while her body shook on the bed.

Peyton already exercised more self-control than she desired, and right now all she wanted to do was brutally lick Stella's pussy.

Peyton stretched her tongue completely out, licked Stella's pussy from bottom to top, and bit down on her clitoral area as she dove between Stella's broad thighs.

Then, as passion and unbridled emotions took possession of her, she began to move her head up and down while keeping her eyes fixated on Stella's face.

Peyton began to suck Stella's pussy like a savage, and her actions lacked any sense of gravity.

All that was there was an insane want to insert her tongue as deeply as possible into the woman's cunt.

Stella was already inching closer to an explosive climax.

Her body was trembling, and her eyes had rolled back into her brain.

She made a fist with Peyton's hair and began to move her hips in time with his licks.

Stella was aware that she was acting in a pornographic manner, but she didn't care.

She was turning into a slut at the sight of Peyton's exquisite face, her smokey eyes, and her wonderful, nude body between her knees.

Stella yelled, "Fuuuuckkkkkk!" as she crossed her knees and squeezed Peyton's face in between them.

The young cop did not, however, slow down.

As she continued to eat her lover's pussy with the same fervor, Stella began to shoot directly into Peyton's mouth. The blonde-haired, once-shy and straight lady was quickly filling her lips with her fluids.

While Stella had her climax, Peyton slurped and swallowed everything that had entered her mouth while grinning and giggling.

After a little while, Stella's shaking body stopped vibrating, and she was left gasping on the bed with Peyton laying on top of her and staring directly into her eyes.

I've never previously made a lady squirm.

"Be quiet! I am very humiliated!" cried Stella, hiding her face with her hands.

Peyton kissed Stella's hands before carefully removing them from her face to kiss Stella's eyes while muttering, "I think my days of sleeping around with women might just have come to an end."

The two ladies chuckled as Stella said, "I think my days of being a straight woman might have just come to an end as well."

Stay with me tonight, Stella pleaded.

"I was going to even if you hadn't asked," the speaker said.

Stella grinned and gave Peyton a strong embrace while feeling pleased and cheerful. She was blissfully ignorant that her phone had just beeped and that a text message had just arrived from an unknown number asking her how long she could continue to lie to herself. It's not over yet.

Harper, a prison guard, roughly gripped my upper arm as we moved through the ward's musty, smoky hallways. She was tall for a lady, much taller than I was, and she seemed like she enjoyed working out. Next to her, I've always felt tiny. The majority of the other female inmates said she always had a gloomy expression on her face, but I knew differently. Given that her dark blonde hair was pulled back behind her in a neat ponytail, she looked particularly nice today. Her blue eyes were set in an even more agitated look than usual after an earlier conflict. I was eager to get to where we were heading because the tight hold on my arm and the shackles behind my back were nourishment for my already ravenous pussy.

We moved together as one amid the ominous cacophony of women screaming and hefty metal gates clanging. She was escorting me to the warden so I could explain why I got involved in the brawl at lunch with two other prisoners. I was unaware of their disagreement. Only when I saw Harper enter the room did I begin to take advantage of the circumstance. I intentionally spilled my leftover milk over Sharon's head so she would see.

Before she double timed it and saved me from her erratic blows, I got the opportunity to observe her eyes get dimmer and a momentary smile cross her face. She told me I had to answer to the warden for continually picking fights in front of all the other prisoners. Since then, my pussy has been sopped.

When we reached the administrative wing, the commotion significantly subsided. I caught a glimpse of my mirror as I passed by a dark office and was pleased to see that my long black hair flowed down my back and that my figure seemed especially slender now that I had increased my gym routines. The warden cared deeply about my health, so she made sure I had as much time as I needed in the gym. After all, prison food was bad for your figure.

As we passed, the secretary's lips pursed. I winked at her while grinning. I'm not sure whether she didn't like me because she believed I was the worst prisoner in the minimal security facility or if it was because she knew something about what happened in the warden's office.

Sometimes Harper wasn't fast enough to make me vomit. My guard gave me a brief tap, and Warden Foxx abruptly said, "Enter," so we entered.

Behind us, Harper closed and secured the door. Behind her desk, the warden was sitting with a hurt expression on her face. She put the phone to her ear, raised her hand, and made the chitter-chatter sound with her fingers to indicate that the person on the other end was talking too much.

Harper escorted me over and pushed my head down beneath the phone wire to give me room to crawl when Foxx slid back her chair. Foxx rolled back as soon as she saw that I was on my knees under the desk with my wrists still bound behind my back, and she immediately undid her jeans to pull them down her legs.

She hurriedly slid her panties and trousers down her legs till they were wrapped around her ankles since she knew

I couldn't use my hands. When I saw her hot pussy inches from my lips, I was unable to stop the grin from spreading over my face. I eagerly began tracing my tongue across her smooth, velour lips. I carefully dropped my lips towards her pussy and licked all over like a horned animal, being careful not to hit my head on the bottom of her desk.

I didn't mind that her musty smell lingered at the back of my nose. I like the taste of her pussy's moisture. Every time I stood up to take a breath, I lapped at the clit's emerging tip.

Above me, the phone discussion went on. It has to do with spending plans and employee turnover rates. agonizingly dull. I questioned if the person on the other end had observed Foxx's voice get a little deeper and pant a little. I imagined the woman above me to have light brown hair, professional eyewear, and green eyes that were becoming dark with want as a result of what the female at her desk was doing to her.

Do you honestly believe that we need to go through each thing line by line right now? She said, her voice filled with resentment and fury.

The person on the other end must not have cared, based on the loud sigh I overheard. I hid my face between her legs and slipped my tongue in and out of her wetness as I tried to cheer her up. Given my circumstance, it wasn't simple, but I succeeded. I was aware that instead of my genuine enthusiasm for her lovely pussy, she would assume that I was attempting to lick my way out of the beating I was about to get.

When my tongue encircled her clit, she moaned. I grinned as I tickled her with the tip of my tongue while leaning back a bit and saw her leg shake.

"No, I simply got a cramp in a hurry. She urged, attempting to conceal her groan with, "Go on.

I devoured her, wishing I had my hands free from my restraints so I could play within her pussy while I enjoyed the flavor and feel of her on my lips. It was unfortunate that she was unaware of what I was capable of doing with my hands.

"On mute."

She pushed the chair back and reached beneath the desk to pull me out by my hair a split second after I heard the automatic voice on her phone tell me that she had turned on the mute option. When she rose and pulled me up, I fell into her and hit my head on the way out. After a few period of time, she had me hunched over her desk and was pulling down the light blue scrub-style trousers they had given us to wear. Those trousers' elastic was so worn-out that it barely held them up. I wasn't wearing any underpants. Always, it made things simpler.

Harper was standing at attention across the room, and I could see him. The warden retrieved my favorite toy—a large pink strap on dildo—from a neighboring drawer as he was doing so. She activated the vibrator and swiftly secured the strap around her hips. The instant I felt her buzzing cock brush against my pussy lips, my hands balled into tight fists. When I finally concentrated my gaze on the guard across from me, she finally eased within my sopping pussy.

Foxx was muttering behind me, "Mm, so fucking wet."

Foxx fucked me on her desk while the phone's droning noise continued. She didn't use any techniques, and she didn't give a damn whether it was comfortable for me or not. She would ram the vibrator into me, groan hornily, and grind her own pussy against the buzzing harness before pulling back and repeating the process. She treated me like nothing more than a fuck toy. But because to my perversions, I was able to take complete enjoyment in things that most women would find repulsive.

The whole situation reminded me of a low-budget pornographic film, but it struck me in every fantasia I indulged in when I wasn't able to get myself into trouble. Additionally, I had Harper to look forward to when the warden finished dealing with me. Even though I adored the rudimentary, animalistic way Foxx used me, she was only the prelude, a method to prolong the suspense. My tits sprang forward against her desk when she gave me a strong buck of the hips.

The warden received a call from someone who had a query. She quickly stopped pushing me and picked up the phone.

"Excuse me, could you say that again?" She enquired as the strap buzzed softly inside of me. She had a really firm hold on my hips.

I blew my hair out of my face and licked my lips as I winked at the security man. She always waited for the warden to finish fiddling with me before she turned, but I would like it if she smothered me with her pussy as he did. She ignored my request and just stared at me.

I had a gut feeling that I would be receiving a few more blows with her government-issued belt for making fun of her.

The warden could only gently enter and exit my tight pussy since she had to engage in the talk. My muscles surrounding the vibrator became more tense, but it was still insufficient for me, and I moaned in despair.

The faraway voice on the phone said, "What was that?"

"Nothing."

Harper retrieved a handkerchief from her pocket and approached the desk when the warden signaled her to do so. I dutifully opened my lips for the gag even though I knew what was about to happen. She grabbed beneath me and firmly squeezed one of my nipples once she got it tightly knotted around my head. Although I moaned, the gag muffled it. The guard returned to her position after finishing her brief exam.

As the very slow and delicate fucking went on, I leaned back, closed my eyes, and tilted my head to the side. I pondered how I got there as my body gently swayed on the desk, three months into a five-month sentence.

I've always had strange sexual inclinations. I would be fucking at least one instructor while I was at school, if not more. No matter whether they were male or female. I was content as long as they utilized their control over me to influence me to do what they wanted. I guess I was a feminist's worst nightmare, but I didn't care as long as it got me on my knees eating a wet pussy on the steps during a dance or sucking cock in an empty classroom.

Because part of the fun for me was getting them to do what I wanted without their understanding it, it would have ruined the illusion for me if they realized how much I wanted them.

I taught my employers my methods after I graduated from college. I never did anything really wrong, but just enough to need several one-on-one meetings.

Then there was the time I offered to let anybody use any of my holes to try to avoid getting a ticket. I was arrested for trying to bribe a police officer and exceeding the speed limit by 50 miles per hour, and the officer became redder than anybody I had ever seen. So there I was, hunched over a desk, still smiling.

The warden's hold on my hips became tighter, and I could feel her trying to screw me more forcefully while maintaining a calm, steady voice. She finally gave up.

Myles, there's been a development. I will need to call you again.

She hung up the phone before waiting for a response. A split second later, she was hammering me so hard that the desk began to jerkily slide across the floor.

She remarked, extending her hand to grasp a hold of my hair and tugging it back. "That's more like it," she said.

Uncomfortably, my head was jerked back, but I couldn't have cared less since my pussy was suddenly receiving the attention it so desperately desired. My stiff nipples brushed against the desk through the thin cotton shirt I was wearing. Given how loud the sound of flesh smacking skin was, I questioned the point of gagged me. Sometimes she would stop pushing and let go of my hair to grasp handfuls of my ass and grip so hard that bruises would appear. After a night like this, I often admired her work in the bathroom mirror.

I sensed a signal in my mind that let me know she wasn't stopping to adjust her grip this time. She undid the strap and inserted her fingers inside the little opening in my shirt. She reached inside her purse and began rubbing her now-slick fingers into my puckered asshole. My teeth dug into my lip, and I whimpered like a little child.

Foxx never truly injured me, but whenever she went for my ass, it stung like the dickens. Making the hole large enough for her dildo to fit was all that mattered to her. She didn't care how much the work she was performing hurt and burned. The reality was, however, that I didn't want it to affect her. If it did, I wouldn't be able to combine that hurt with my own special combination of spicy kink to create a mouthwatering dish of scalding desire.

When she had sufficiently stretched me, she pulled her fingers back and pushed the vibrator into my butt. She pushed me up by reaching beneath me before she began thrusting. Her hands firmly fisted my tits after locking onto them. Although the discomfort made my eyes water, I was grateful for the new angle that had my clit rubbing against the edge of the desk as she began pounding the dildo in and out. Every time the vibrating harness rubbed against her pussy, the warden let out breathy groans.

I immediately found the ideal posture while perched on my toes. Every time she pushed into me, I gripped and unclenched my pussy while clenching my eyes tight and leaning back. I didn't take long to be ready to come thanks to her cock inside of me, the desk's rough wood on my clit, and the tightness of my muscles.

Sadly, she did it before me. When she sank into my little hole one final time, she stopped making strong thrusts and her hold tightened painfully as she shouted out her climax and pressed her pelvis into my pert ass. As I felt her body trembling against me, tears were in my eyes. Her hips surged in closer, squeezing the strap into my tightly wound torso as it buzzed within.

My upper body collapsed onto her desk as she suddenly let go of my tits since I was unable to brace myself with my hands behind me due to the cuffs. She snatched the cock out of my ass and gave me a casual slap on the behind while telling Harper, "I'm gonna go get cleaned up and then you can belt her."

I was panting profusely as I rested against the desk and listened to the warden traverse the office to her private restroom in high heels. I turned my head to look across the room and saw the guard take off her belt from the loops. On a bench next to her, every piece of hardware that was attached to it was positioned with care.

She looked at my ass like a hungry beast as she was getting ready. I pondered if the warden's fingerprints left her feeling inspired or wishing she had a fresh canvas on which to paint. Harper never fucked me outside the warden's office, though, and the warden never let her go first. I couldn't help but believe that she was drawn to sloppy seconds.

When Foxx returned, she delivered my body to Harper and sat in a chair in front of her window on the second floor, giving her a great view of my impending belt lashing. She left her jeans undone and tucked them halfway down her thighs since she knew it wouldn't be long before she was ready to go again. I offered her a quick grin since I knew she enjoyed seeing little girls being pounded up with big belts.

Foxx never spoke to me, but the guard was the complete opposite.

She tightened the strap, "I don't know what the hell we're going to do with you," she said. "For one reason or another, you come in here almost every week. The last time you came back, my belt's stripes weren't even entirely faded.

She moved her hands over my broad ass as though looking for evidence of the pounding I had received.

"Every time I criticize you, I hope that you'll eventually grow up. But here you are once again.

She stopped. I knew it was my signal to answer. "Ma'am, I'm really sorry. I'm not sure what affects me. My voice trembled at the appropriate spots.

Even though I craved her belt on my skin more than ever, a sizable part of me continued to fear and dread the suffering each strike would cause. My terror wasn't just an act. She beat me harder and harder every time she disciplined me, pushing me to the edge and trying my skin's durability.

My hot pussy was moist as her hand slipped between my legs, her fingers gliding through it. As she continued to lecture, she swiped it on my behind.

"I believe it is my personal responsibility to make sure you leave here transformed and with a clearer grasp of what is required of you in the outside world. You may be sure that I will beat your ass till it is raw and bleeding if necessary.

Although she had not yet inflicted even the tiniest rip in my skin, she had previously made the same threat. The words continue to cause me to tremble with both want and anxiety. I wailed against the gag while clenching my fists.

Instead of flogging me as I had anticipated, she proceeded to go further between my thighs and toyed with my hot pussy. Before the beating, at least, she had never experienced this. My clit, however, was by no means unexplored ground for her, and she immediately had me writhing against the desk as she toyed with it.

She stopped as soon as I began to moan, my climax only a pinch away, and instead gave me a hard smack on the pussy.

My mouth was choked, but I still managed to squeak a sound into the space. Before I could calm myself, Harper slammed the belt down firmly on my ass with a booming smack as the two ladies giggled at my wrath.

It energized the space.

She put a stripe of fire on me, and I shrieked, my cheeks clenching together. This wasn't some kind of low-key BDSM play performed in the privacy of one's bedroom. Harper wanted to really harm me. She had no time to catch her breath before her belt began to whistle again. Even though my pussy was buzzing with pleasure and excitement, I writhed and twisted, seeking to escape the torture. But she had no trouble holding me down as she repeatedly struck me. I could see Foxx slipping her finger into her pussy through my thrashing; the sight of me being thrashed was a huge turn on for her.

She said, "Again," becoming irritated when Harper paused too long between punches.

The belt dropped, and the quick firing came one after another. The agony was excruciating, and I could feel myself beginning to freak out, wondering if maybe this was the moment when everything would get out of hand. It was at this point that my capacity to get pleasure from it would be utterly overtaken by agony. And just as I was about to lose all remaining strength, the pounding halted.

I hardly paid attention when I felt the vibrator separate my pussy lips and descend far into me because I was breathing so forcefully through my nose that I was afraid I may hyperventilate. I broke down in floods of delight as the relief that I had survived the worst beating of my life rushed through me. Even though the guard was holding me just as hard as Foxx had before her, endorphins were permeating my body and swooshing away the heat on my ass.

The warden's pussy rubbed against my lips as my head was pulled up by my hair and the gag was pulled from my mouth. I gaped open and pushed out my tongue hungrily, craving every bodily feeling I could get my hands on.

Foxx began to grind against my face with no less vigor as she did on my ass as she forced her pussy deep on me. She watched as my tongue darted up and down her moist slit while holding my head motionless in her hands and grinning evilly at me. As Harper pressed even more and the dildo stretched me out wide, I groaned in a girlish manner.

The guard used lengthy, forceful strokes to secure the strap, pulling it out almost completely before slamming it shut once again. She fucked with a purpose and passion that I had never experienced with any woman and was very afraid I would never experience again after I was released from jail. After I was freed, I already had some kind of crazy plan to rob a liquor shop so I could return and be raped by her once again. It was just a dream.